"*Releasing Miracles* is an excellent book on the subject. I found it to cover so many valuable issues regarding healing and miracles. I found it biblically balanced and well written. A great book for someone interested in healing for themselves or the ministry of healing for others. Very thorough in the subjects covered and full of great illustrative stories."

Randy Clark, D.D., D.Min., Th.D., author, *Power to Heal*, *Authority to Heal*, *The Healing Breakthrough* and *Eyewitness to Miracles*; president, Global Awakening Theological Seminary, Family of Faith Christian University

"The apostle Paul declared that the Kingdom of God should be expressed not only in word but also in power. In *Releasing Miracles*, my friend Kynan Bridges stirs us to believe for miracles and equips us to *do them*! This book provides necessary tools to launch us into the next levels of releasing miracles."

Robert Henderson, bestselling author, *Operating in the Courts of Heaven* and the Courts of Heaven series

"The Body of Christ today is inundated by books and sermons full of insight, but it is largely ineffective because it does not know how to cooperate with the Holy Spirit to release the power of God. Thankfully, my good friend Kynan Bridges has produced *Releasing Miracles*, a beautiful book that provides a warm and revelatory overview to guide all believers into a powerful life and effective ministry. I encourage you to read it prayerfully and allow God to lead you into a life of real fullness in the Holy Spirit."

Joan Hunter, president, Joan Hunter Ministries; author; TV host, *Miracles Happen*

"Dr. Kynan Bridges tells it like it is in *Releasing Miracles*. Sadly, the Church has left the supernatural and miracles out of the menu, thus leaving the hopeless and sick starving for a power encounter with the Lord. This sad state of affairs has become my personal pet peeve, especially since, as Dr. Kynan teaches, miracles are our

T0327131

portion because of the cross of Christ! Throughout this book, Dr. Kynan lays out the blueprint for healing directly from the Scriptures. He makes it so clear and states it so powerfully that any believer can reproduce the miracles Jesus performed. As one who has administered thousands of miracles, I applaud his work. There are not enough people operating in the fullness of the supernatural power available to us through Jesus. I believe this book can change all that."

Katie Souza, Katie Souza Ministries

RELEASING
MIRACLES

RELEASING
MIRACLES

HOW TO WALK IN THE
SUPERNATURAL POWER OF GOD

KYNAN BRIDGES

Chosen
a division of Baker Publishing Group
Minneapolis, Minnesota

Published by Chosen Books
Minneapolis, Minnesota
ChosenBooks.com

Chosen Books is a division of
Baker Publishing Group, Grand Rapids, Michigan

Printed in the United States of America

Library of Congress Cataloging-in-Publication Data
Names: Bridges, Kynan, author.
Title: Releasing miracles : how to walk in the supernatural power of God / Kynan
   Bridges.
Description: Minneapolis, Minnesota : Chosen Books, a division of Baker
   Publishing Group, [2022]
Identifiers: LCCN 2022023758 | ISBN 9780800762605 (trade paper) | ISBN
   9780800762858 (casebound) | ISBN 9781493437641 (ebook)
Subjects: LCSH: Miracles. | Supernatural. | Power (Christian theology)
Classification: LCC BT97.3 .B75 2022 | DDC 231.7/3—dc23/eng/20220711
LC record available at https://lccn.loc.gov/2022023758

Cover design by Rob Williams, InsideOut Creative Arts, Inc.

Baker Publishing Group publications use paper produced from sustainable forestry practices and postconsumer waste whenever possible.

24   25   26   27   28   29   30   8   7   6   5   4   3   2

I dedicate this work the Lord Jesus Christ,
the reason and purpose for all things.

I also want to dedicate this book to
my beautiful wife, Gloria Bridges (aka SugarBoo Wifey).
Without you, this book and all books I have written would be
impossible. I love you more than words can express.

To my children, thank you for being my bedrock;
you are my greatest treasure.

To my supporters and partners, this message is for you.

Contents

Contents

Foreword

Dr. Kynan Bridges has been a frequent guest on my *It's Supernatural!* television show and has served on my board of directors for many years. So I can really say I know him!

Releasing Miracles could well be Kynan's best and most important book. Why? Because we are entering the time when we will witness what Jesus referred to as the "greater works"! "I tell you the truth, anyone who believes in me will do the same works I have done, and even greater works" (John 14:12 NLT).

What will be greater than the blind seeing, the deaf hearing and the dead being raised? How about praying in the amputee ward of a hospital and seeing limbs restored before your very eyes? How about witnessing not just one person rise from the dead, but hundreds in one city at one time? How about laying hands on cancer patients whose flesh was destroyed and watching it be instantly restored? How about seeing this happen live on the secular TV news networks! There will be so much good news, they won't have time for the other!

We need the greater works. The world is too far gone. It is beyond help from politics. It cannot be restored by man. The devil has made his best move—now it's God's turn! He is our only hope. And He is *more than enough*!

I have concentrated on miracles for my entire fifty years of public ministry. Miracles are how Jesus reached the multitudes with the Good News. And miracles are how I reach large numbers of Jewish people today.

Last week I led an outreach meeting in Israel with 950 unsaved Jewish Israelis in attendance. During the meeting, large numbers of these nonbelievers raised their hand to signify they had just been healed! Then well over 900 of them boldly stood up and publicly proclaimed Jesus as Messiah and Lord. Without the miracles this would never have happened! This was as historic as what was recorded in the book of Acts at Pentecost!

The working of miracles was God's number-one method to evangelize the first church. And God has never changed.

We are coming into the greatest harvest of souls in history. The least follower of Jesus in the first church walked in miracles. How much more must we walk in miracles just before His return!

Releasing Miracles is written for evangelicals who have never walked in or even believed in modern-day miracles, as well as for charismatics who believe in miracles but see very few. Kynan teaches first from the Bible, then from firsthand experience. Many will receive a supernatural impartation flowing from the words of this book to walk in miracles.

As miracles are released in this end-time move of God's Spirit, it will galvanize the true Church. God is sending out a shofar-blast mandate worldwide. He is saying, "All hands on deck!" This is God's time for you to walk in the greater works, the greater miracles. It's time for you to be normal—that's normal as defined by the Bible!

Sid Israel Roth, host, *It's Supernatural!*

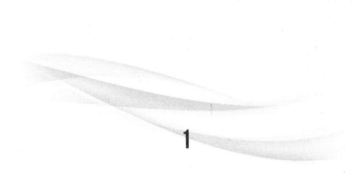

Miracles

Our Spiritual Inheritance

"Most assuredly, I say to you, he who believes in Me, the works that I do he will do also; and greater works than these he will do, because I go to My Father."

John 14:12

As the scorching sun beat upon his face, the noise of the crowd grew as each person pushed their way closer and closer to the pool, growing so loud now that he couldn't even hear himself think. Nor could he move his paralyzed body closer to the pool.

Suddenly, the voices of the multitude dimmed, and a single voice became clearer and clearer. "Will you be made whole?" He asked, His voice so gentle and yet so powerful it could be heard above the noise, as if every other voice faded away. The face of a stranger towering over his frail body seemed so eerily familiar. "Rise, take up your bed, and walk!"

The command was given with such authority, he couldn't even resist.

Immediately, his body began to quake from within, as he could hear the cracking of bone and feel the stretching of his muscle tissues. His ligaments and tendons felt like they were snapping back into place. Suddenly, he stood on his feet—perplexed and yet relieved. After 38 years of paralysis and a stagnant existence by a pool he had never once entered, the man was totally healed and restored. He received a miracle!

This is my own dramatized version of one of my favorite biblical accounts, the story of the man at the pool of Bethesda. I believe it paints the perfect picture of the omnibenevolence of God in performing a miracle for a man who was undeserving. In fact, it is no coincidence that the miracle takes place there, because the word *Bethesda* literally means "house of mercy."[1] Could it be that this miracle of divine restoration paints a vivid picture for us of the underlying purpose for miracles? Let's explore.

Why Miracles?

All my life, I have wondered about God and the supernatural. From the first time I read the Bible, I knew intuitively there must be something more to this world than what I could see with my natural eyes. Unfortunately, when I would speak to other Christians, there wasn't much talk of miracles. Granted, we learned a lot about the moral responsibilities of Christians (e.g., *don't lie, don't steal, don't cheat, don't chew or hang with those who do*). It was, however, a strange thing to ask someone, "How many miracles did you experience today?" And even if you asked that question, some would respond by saying, "The fact that I am still breathing is a miracle!," or "Every day is a miracle!" With this I would agree to an extent. There is nothing wrong with seeing every day as a miracle, but if we are going to be faithful to the Word of God, we need to acknowledge that God had a specific definition in mind when He introduced the concept of miracles in Scripture. So before we can answer the question, *Why miracles?*, you may be wondering, *What are miracles?* I am very glad that you asked. The Bible says that Jesus of Nazareth was "approved" of God by miracles, signs and wonders. "Ye men of Israel, hear these words; Jesus of Nazareth, a man approved of God among you by miracles and wonders and signs, which God did by him in the midst of you, as ye yourselves also know" (Acts 2:22 KJV). The word *approved* here comes from the Greek word *apodeiknymi*, which means to point away from oneself, to show forth, to expose to view or to prove by demonstration.[2] In other words, Jesus' ministry was filled with miracles, and these miracles pointed people to the King and His Kingdom, demonstrating His power. The word for *miracles* here is rendered from the Greek word *dynamis*, which literally means demonstrative power, dynamic power or the power to perform miracles. In the ancient world, power had to be demonstrated in order to confirm the truth and veracity of that power. If God is real, He must possess the ability to perform miracles. Another definition of a miracle according to the *Oxford Dictionary* is "a surprising and welcome event that is not explicable by natural or scientific laws and is therefore considered to be the work of a divine agency."[3] I like to define a miracle as an intervention, interruption or overriding of natural laws by God—or when eternity invades time.

The Argument for Miracles

The presence of miracles is proof (from a logical and philosophical standpoint) that God is real. Why? If God is a supernatural being, then the presence of the supernatural points to the reality of God. Furthermore, how can anyone claim to follow a supreme being who is incapable of affecting the natural world? If God is omnipotent, then He must have the ability to heal disease and raise the dead. These are the very things that characterized the ministry of Jesus. Again, Acts 2:22 tells us that Jesus was "approved of God" by signs and wonders. The question would be, Are our churches today approved by the same standard as the first-century Church? I believe that where miracles begin, arguments end. The truth is, this generation longs for an authentic display of the presence and power of God. People don't just want to hear about the God of the Bible; they want to experience Him in a very real and tangible way. I believe there is a clarion call to the Church to walk in and release the miraculous power of God on a daily basis.

We said earlier that a miracle is defined as an intervention in or an overriding of a natural law or process. According to this definition, miracles happen when heaven literally invades the earth. Every time a miracle takes place, the sovereignty and love of God are established in the hearts and minds of the recipients or witnesses to those miracles. Glory to God! The crack addicts on the street may not understand systematic theology, but they understand being delivered from the power of addiction. The prostitute on the corner or the woman being trafficked may not know anything about hermeneutics or homiletics, but she knows what it means to be liberated from the power of perversion. Unfortunately, many well-meaning Christians (including spiritual leaders) have participated in the "Great Omission." They have omitted the power of God from the Gospel. By doing so, they have effectively removed God from the Gospel, and if He is omitted, then all you have left is a "spell." Many people in the American church are under the spell of intellectualism, which has given birth to a powerless Christianity. The good news is that millions of Christians all over the world are experiencing a hunger for the supernatural power of God.

What Does Love Look Like?

What if I told you that the Bible was not simply a theological book or a historical record of the ancient world? Yes. The Bible does contain those things, but I believe the Bible is so much more. I believe that the Bible is literally an open letter to humanity, articulating the heart and mind of God. More specifically, I believe that the Gospel is a love story to humankind, and this love story was demonstrated through the greatest miracle in the history of the world: the incarnation, death, burial and resurrection of our Messiah, Jesus Christ. Think about this for a moment. The greatest story ever told is a love story that is essentially a story of miracles.

Miracles are a manifestation of God's love for the human race. God redeemed humanity because He loves humanity (see John 3:16). God heals humanity because He loves humanity. God reveals Himself through miracles to humanity because He loves humanity.

The Gospel is a love story to humankind, and the demonstration of that love is miracles.

The question when it comes to miracles is, "What does love look like?" To the man at the pool of Bethesda who had been in that condition for 38 years, love looked like, "Rise, take up your mat and walk!" Can you imagine the joy he experienced? Can you imagine the look on his face? If you told that man that God loved him, do you think he would believe it? To the Samaritan woman, trapped in a life of immorality, love looked like a conversation at the well with Jesus, where the secrets of her heart were revealed and a radical face-to-face encounter with the Messiah took place. In a moment, her life was supernaturally transformed because she received "living water." To a young man sitting in his living room watching Christian television and listening to a televangelist talk about the Holy Spirit, love looked like experiencing God come into His living room and radically saving him and filling him with the Holy Ghost. (That young man was me!)

If you are reading this book, you are part of a remnant of believers who will actively partner and participate in what I believe to be the next great move of God. This is not some dramatic statement inserted for emotional effect; this is a sincere and genuine declaration for what I believe to be the heart of God for this generation. Miracles are not just random occurrences, or spontaneous manifestations of an impersonal "Universe," but they are the deliberate displays of love by an omnibenevolent God—an "all-good" God. They are, indeed, our inheritance.

Miracles Are Our Portion

Merriam-Webster defines an *inheritance* as (1) "the act of getting by legal right from a person at his or her death or through heredity"; (2) "something gotten by legal right from a person at his or her death."[4] In short, Jesus died to give us a spiritual inheritance. Scripture speaks of this very explicitly.

> "Most assuredly, I say to you, he who believes in Me, the works that I do he will do also; and greater works than these he will do, because I go to My Father."
>
> John 14:12

We are empowered to do what Jesus did. Why? "Because I go unto the Father." Jesus' journey to the Father began with the cross. The cross was the doorway He went through in order to fulfill God's plan of redemption. As a result, He (Jesus) has given us His Spirit, so that the same works that He did, we would also do. What were the works that Jesus did? "God anointed Jesus of Nazareth with the Holy Spirit and with power," and Jesus "went about doing good and healing all who were oppressed by the devil, for God was with Him" (Acts 10:38).

Jesus worked miracles. He healed the sick. He expelled demons. Those were the works that He did. If we are supposed to do what He did and greater, then we, too, should be walking in the supernatural power of God. In fact, the Bible says, "And these signs will follow those who believe: In My name they will cast out demons; they will speak with new tongues" (Mark 16:17).

What would happen if you and I thought about miracles as our portion or inheritance rather than something we performed? *Inheritance* implies heredity. In other words, the miraculous is inextricably connected to our born-again nature in Christ. (We will explore this in more detail later.) Just like anything you inherit, acknowledgment and recognition are necessary in order to release the portion that has been given to you.

Increased Awareness Increases Authority

I have realized in my journey in the miraculous that the more you are aware of who He is, who you are and what you possess on the inside, the more authority you have to operate in miracles.

Jesus asked a profound question in the gospel account found in Matthew 16:13: "When Jesus came into the region of Caesarea Philippi, He asked His disciples, saying, 'Who do men say that I, the Son of Man, am?'"

Jesus posed this question in a significant place, Caesarea Philippi. This was a popular site of the renowned temple of Pan in the first century. People came from all over the Roman Empire to worship idols. We don't have any evidence for this, but I am willing to bet that it was probably very crowded and loud when Jesus posed this question. There is something prophetic about that potential detail alone. Who do people say Jesus is in the midst of all the cultural "noise" around us? What do people perceive Him to be? But the second question is even more profound than the first: "He said to them, 'But who do you say that I am?'" (verse 15).

Jesus wanted to know who His disciples perceived Him to be. Was He simply one of the prophets? Was He John the Baptist reincarnated? Did they share the same sentiments of the masses who watched Him from afar? Then Peter stood up and exclaimed,

"You are the Christ, the Son of the living God" (verse 16). To this Jesus responded,

> "Blessed are you, Simon Bar-Jonah, for flesh and blood has not revealed this to you, but My Father who is in heaven. And I also say to you that you are Peter, and on this rock I will build My church, and the gates of Hades shall not prevail against it. And I will give you the keys of the kingdom of heaven, and whatever you bind on earth will be bound in heaven, and whatever you loose on earth will be loosed in heaven."
>
> verses 17–19

The revelation of the person of Jesus was (and is) an essential ingredient to the foundation of the Church and the authority of the believer. Jesus referred to *keys*. This is the Greek word *kleis*, denoting power and authority of various kinds. In other words, there is a correlation between revelation and authority. The greater the revelation of who Jesus is, the greater the authority to release His power. This is why the question of, "Who do you say I am?" is so important. If Jesus is simply a theological concept, then that is all we will be able to offer people. But if He truly is the Christ (the Anointed One and His anointing) who is the source of all miracles, then we will be able to offer the miraculous to everyone around us.

A Personal Story of a Miracle

My wife shared a very powerful testimony with me of a miracle that she received. Several years ago, she was diagnosed with a cyst on her ovaries. The doctors gave her a very negative prognosis. But my wife is a woman of great faith and expectancy. She determined in herself that she was going to receive a miracle from God. Every day she came to church she would declare that the cyst on her ovaries was dissolved. During the teaching, she would feel a burning sensation in her ovaries. This was not a painful burning, but it felt like the fire of God was burning up the cyst. This went on for several weeks, until one day, she went to the doctor, and he confirmed that the cyst had totally disappeared. Glory to God! There are times when people will go to a miracle crusade and have a powerful healing evangelist lay hands on them, and they will experience a supernatural healing. Those are awesome experiences. But God can move supernaturally through what we would call "everyday people." No one laid hands on my wife to receive a miracle, yet she released her faith for the miraculous because she believed with all her heart that the miraculous is her inheritance; you should believe the same for you!

Miracles Are Your Right

One of things that I often hear when speaking to many well-meaning Christians is that God will do something for us "if it's His will." I have heard this statement literally thousands of times. Trust me when I say I know the heart behind this statement. It is an effort to acknowledge the sovereignty of God. Please understand that the sovereignty of God will never abdicate the authority of the believer, nor will it remove our spiritual rights as citizens in the Kingdom of God. This is one of the most foundational truths that you must understand if you are to live in a sustained flow of the power and presence of God. As audacious as it may sound, you must know that a miracle doesn't just take place because God is in a particular mood on a particular day. On the contrary, miracles are a part of a spiritual inheritance given to us through Jesus and His efficacious work on the cross. The moment you and I were born again, we received the same Spirit that raised Jesus from the dead, and therefore we have received the same *dynamis* power (the power to perform miracles). I know that comment may make some conservative theologians turn over in their graves, but I can assure you that it is absolutely scriptural. Every believer has been given the divine right to operate in the miraculous.

Next, I'd like to draw our attention to Ephesians 3:20: "Now to Him who is able to do exceedingly abundantly above all that we ask or think, according to the power that works in us." Did you notice that the apostle Paul says explicitly that God's ability to "do exceedingly abundantly above all that we ask or think" is according to "the power that works in us"?

Every believer has been given the divine right to operate in the miraculous.

There are two words I want to expound upon in this text. The first is the word *according*, derived from the Greek word *kata*—an interesting word, which can be rendered "down from" or "throughout." Now, when you read it in that context, it gives the passage a different meaning. God is able to do exceedingly abundantly above all we can ask or think "down from" the power that works in us. God's omnipotent ability flows down from or throughout the power that works in us. This brings me to the second word that I would like to define in this text. The word *power* comes from the Greek word *dynamis*, which literally means miracle-working power, or the power to perform miracles, or the power resident in a thing by virtue of its nature. In other words, God's ability to work for us or through us is inextricably connected to the measure of His power working in us.

Imagine that a wealthy businessman bought a Bugatti sports car (valued at over one million dollars) and this sports car was capable of reaching 200 miles per hour, with an engine capable of 1,000 horsepower. Now imagine that this businessman only drove the car back and forth to work in stop-and-go traffic or on residential streets with a speed limit of 35 miles per hour. It would be safe to say that he is not maximizing the full potential of the vehicle. Why? Even though his car is capable of massive amounts of power, his gas pedal is only demanding minimal amounts of power from the engine because of his driving habits. Now imagine that this same driver was given the opportunity to drive on the Autobahn in Germany or an open highway in Dubai or the salt flats of Utah, would he experience a totally different vehicle?

In many ways, we have been given access to operate in the unlimited power of God, yet many Christians are stuck in spiritual traffic, only seeing a limited measure of what God desires to do in and through them. They have yet to put their "pedal to the metal" and release the supernatural power of God, so they are experiencing small doses of the supernatural, rather than the deluge they have inherited in Christ.

SUMMARY QUESTIONS

1. What are miracles, and why are they important?
2. How do miracles demonstrate God's love for humanity?
3. Why does every believer have the divine right to operate in miracles?
4. What does our spiritual inheritance in Christ include?

MIRACLE ACTIVATION

Father, in the name of Jesus, I thank You for the inheritance that I have received in Christ. I thank You that You have given me the miraculous as a divine birthright. I will walk in the full expression of this divine birthright. Thank You for the working of Your mighty power in and through me in a way that brings You honor. Let people experience Your presence through the words that I speak and the actions that I take. From today forward, I will receive my inheritance. I embrace the truth that I am Your child, and as Your child, Your Spirit operates in and through me to the glory of Your name. Holy Spirit, have Your way in my life in Jesus' name. Amen!

2

Jesus

The Blueprint of the Miraculous

And it came to pass on a certain day, as he was teaching, that there were Pharisees and doctors of the law sitting by, which were come out of every town of Galilee, and Judaea, and Jerusalem: and the power of the Lord was present to heal them.

Luke 5:17 KJV

Crowds gathered around the house. There were so many people that you could hardly see beyond the person standing in front of you. As the multitudes pressed closer and closer to the house, they could hear the One so many had spoken about. The Rabbi was teaching.

Suddenly, you could hear the sound of wood breaking above the place where the Master was teaching. The knocking sound grew louder and louder as light broke in from the ceiling. What was happening?

The strangest thing had just taken place. A paralytic man was let down through the roof as a deafening silence pierced the atmosphere. The Messiah gazed at the man with an unbroken stare as hundreds watched to see what He would say. A palpable presence hovered over the crowd.

"Man, your sins are forgiven you," the Messiah said with a serious face.[1]

Now the silence had turned into the sporadic sounds of shock by the religious leaders.

Before the crowd could gather themselves, the Messiah said,

"Which is easier, to say, 'Your sins are forgiven you,' or to say, 'Rise up and walk'? But that you may know that the Son of Man has power on earth to forgive sins." Then He told the paralyzed man, "I say to you, arise, take up your bed, and go to your house."[2]

Immediately, the man who was let down through the roof by his faithful friends took up his mat and walked for the first time since anyone could remember. How was this possible? What manner of man was this?

Understanding the Blueprint

I can only imagine the scene of the miracle recorded in the gospel of Luke. The man with the "palsy" was forever changed by the healing power of the Christ. How did this miracle impact his life? How did it affect the atmosphere? What happened in the hearts and minds of the onlookers? These are questions we may not often ask when reading biblical accounts such as this one, but these are not simply anecdotal stories from ancient folklore; these are real-life accounts of real people who encountered a very real God.

So far, we have talked about the fact that miracles are not simply sporadic occurrences, but are part of our spiritual inheritance as New Testament believers. Every miracle ever done by our Lord left an indelible mark on those who received them. As we continue along this line of understanding the purpose, power and practical keys to releasing the miraculous, it is important for us to gain a greater insight into the spiritual blueprint that God has established in His Word for miracles. Everything in the Kingdom of God follows a spiritual blueprint. What do I mean by this? I am very glad you asked!

A blueprint is defined as a design plan or other technical drawing. It is essentially a schematic or framework for something that allows that thing to be reproduced the way it was originally intended. Another way of looking at a blueprint is by thinking of it as a pattern.

For example, in Exodus 25:8–9, God said this to Moses: "And let them make Me a sanctuary, that I may dwell among them. According to all that I show you, that is, the pattern of the tabernacle and the pattern of all its furnishings, just so you shall make it." This is a very profound spiritual principle. God instructed Moses to build a sanctuary according to the pattern of the tabernacle. What pattern was he referring to? The Bible answers this question in verse 40 of the same chapter: "And see to it that you make them according to the pattern which was shown you on the mountain." God showed Moses a heavenly pattern when he was on Mount Sinai for forty days and forty nights. This means that everything that was built on the earth was built according to the pattern that had already been established in heaven. In other words, the heavenly tabernacle was the blueprint for the earthly tabernacle.

On Earth as in Heaven

Jesus made a very powerful statement in response to the request of His disciple Philip to show him the Father: "Have I been with you so long, and yet you have not known Me, Philip? He who has seen Me has seen the Father; so how can you say, 'Show us the Father'?" (John 14:9).

These words of Jesus are a theological game changer. Jesus tells us that He is the express image of the Father (see Hebrews 1:3). If we want to know the nature, character and heart of the Father, all we need to do is look at Jesus, because Jesus is the embodiment of the spiritual blueprint of heaven. He is the pattern. He is the example. In fact, Jesus tells us that He only does what He sees the Father do. "Then Jesus answered and said to them, 'Most assuredly, I say to you, the Son can do nothing of Himself, but what He sees the Father do; for whatever He does, the Son also does in like manner'" (John 5:19).

Jesus not only follows the blueprint, but He is the blueprint. He looks at the Father and demonstrates His love by performing miracles, and we must look at Jesus and demonstrate His love by releasing miracles. This is why Jesus said in the model prayer found in Matthew 6:10, "Your kingdom come. Your will be done on earth as it is in heaven."

Just as Moses was given the pattern in heaven and instructed to reproduce on earth what he saw in heaven, we as the Church are called to release miracles according to the pattern, which is Jesus Himself.

Jesus Is Our Example

Jesus is the spiritual template for what is possible and how to release miracles. Jesus shows us who the Father is by doing what the Father does. The declaration "On earth as it is in heaven" is a clarion call to the Church to walk out the reality of the miraculous according to the divine blueprint which is already established in the heavenly realm.

As much as some would like to assert, "It's not about miracles! It's about the Gospel!," the reality is that Jesus' ministry was characterized by the miraculous. If it is about the Gospel of Christ, as so many claim, then what the apostle Paul declared in Romans 1:16 should be at the very core of our theology: "For I am not ashamed of the gospel of Christ, for it is the power of God to salvation for everyone who believes, for the Jew first and also for the Greek. " The Bible says that the Gospel of Christ is the very source of the *dynamis* (or miracle-working) power of God. Inextricably connected to the Gospel is the power to perform miracles. So when people say it is about the Gospel, they are absolutely right, but at the center of the Gospel is "the power of God to salvation" (Romans 1:16 KJV). There is a condition to that statement in Scripture: "for everyone who believes."

Do you believe it?

Access Has Been Granted

What if I told you that the doors you have been waiting on to open in your spiritual life have already been opened? How would that change the way you approach the things of God? How would that change the way you pray? You would probably have more confidence and more authority in your spiritual life. Guess what? The door to the miraculous was opened two thousand years ago. That's right! You are not waiting on God to "use you" (a concept I will address in a later chapter), but God is waiting on you to simply believe and walk in the reality He has already made available for us. What are we supposed to believe? The Gospel! The moment we accept the truth that we have received a supernatural inheritance in Christ that we must walk out by faith, is the moment our lives will be radically changed. It's like a person standing in front of a key access door with a key on their hip waiting for the door to swing open on its own. What would be the problem with that scenario? They have the key, but they aren't utilizing it, because they are waiting for something to happen outside of their control. They believe that the door will open if it "be His holy will." Nothing could be further from the truth! Friends, access has already been granted, but we must place a demand on what Jesus has already done.

I want this to really sink down into your spirit: Access has been granted! What does that statement mean? *Access* is defined as a means of approaching or entering a place. In other words, we don't have to be spiritual window shoppers. We don't have to be passive spectators or onlookers in spiritual matters. We can enter into the house and experience all that the Father has graciously provided for us. Glory to God!

The Mystery of John 14:12

In the gospel of John, chapter 14, we see a great spiritual mystery. Jesus told His disciples, "Most assuredly, I say to you, he who believes in Me, the works that I do he will do also; and greater works than these he will do, because I go to My Father" (verse 12).

If there were a list of some of the most controversial verses in the Bible, John 14:12 would definitely be included. Essentially, the Messiah said that those who believe in Him would do the same works that He does, and greater. That is a profound statement. Notice that it gives the condition "he who believes." Believing is the qualifier to operate in the works of Jesus. It is also important to note that Jesus does not say "the works that I did"; He said "the works that I do." Why is that a significant detail? In most accurate word-to-word translations from the original Greek—including the English Standard Version, the New American Standard Bible, the Christian Standard Bible, etc.—this detail is brought out. Jesus has never stopped doing the work. The miracle-working power of God is not simply a matter of historical record; it is a present-day reality through the power of the Holy Spirit. How is this the case? Jesus tells us later in the same verse, "because I go to the Father."

The Person of the Holy Spirit is still working today through us. He is still releasing miracles today! Could it be possible that this generation can and will see greater miracles than those Jesus manifested during his time on earth as the Son of Man? The first-century Church recorded miracles that were never recorded during the earthly ministry of Jesus (e.g., Peter's shadow healing people, a snake biting Paul and him not dying, handkerchiefs being used to cast out demons). But I believe the greater works are the manifestation of the power of the Holy Spirit through an entire body of believers, rather than just a handful of people. The Holy Spirit is Jesus without boundaries. Glory to God!

The Spiritual Key of Compassion

One of the most powerful keys to releasing miracles as exemplified by our Lord is the key of compassion. The Bible says, "But when He saw the multitudes, He was moved with compassion for them, because they were weary and scattered, like sheep having no shepherd" (Matthew 9:36). Jesus was moved with compassion. The word *compassion* in this verse comes from the Greek word *splagchnizomai*, which means to be moved as to one's bowels, hence to be moved with compassion, have compassion (for the bowels were thought to be the seat of love and pity). The *Oxford Dictionary* defines compassion as "sympathetic pity and concern for the sufferings or misfortunes of others." Simply put, Jesus was moved by the sufferings of others. This was a means through which the power and presence of God was released to heal those who were sick and broken.

Ironically, this is what introduced me to the ministry of healing. I saw so many people suffering unnecessarily. I had loved ones who died prematurely from sickness and disease. This caused me to search the Word of God for hours and study every Scripture I could on divine healing. Since that time, we have seen thousands healed and restored by the supernatural power of God. I have come to realize that compassion is a key to releasing the miraculous.

How do we develop a heart of compassion? Jesus spent time praying. We must spend time in prayer so that we can cultivate the heart of God. There is a connection between love and miracles.

Testimony of a Compassion Miracle

Years ago, I was ministering at a large church. After the ministry session, as I was still standing at the altar, the Lord instructed me to pray for every Native American person in attendance at the time. I wasn't sure why at first, but I asked the pastor if I could pray for the various Native American tribes represented in his congregation, and he was in total agreement. Suddenly, a spirit of compassion came over me. I began to feel the pain and the emotional trauma that so many in the room had been dealing with for years. I began to weep and repent on behalf of all those in authority and influence who had abused or mistreated those precious people. All of a sudden, you could hear the cries of the people. They began to wail as the presence of God filled the room. As we continued to pray, I opened the altar, and many people began to come forward for prayer. Immediately, chronic illnesses were healed. Arthritis was healed. Fibromyalgia was healed. The more the atmosphere was filled with compassion, the more miracles began to break out all over the church. It was absolutely amazing.

Being Led by the Spirit

> Then Jesus, being filled with the Holy Spirit, returned from the Jordan and was led by the Spirit into the wilderness.
>
> Luke 4:1

This brings me to a very important spiritual truth: Jesus always followed the leading of the Holy Spirit. We must be led by the Holy Spirit continually. You may ask what this has to do with miracles. Everything! The Bible says, "For as many as are led by the Spirit of God, these are sons of God" (Romans 8:14). If you are going to grow and flow in miracles, you must learn to surrender your will to God and allow the Holy Spirit to lead you. This is the marker of spiritual sonship.

Have you ever woken up in the morning and asked the Holy Spirit, "What are we doing today?" Have you ever allowed God to lead you to do something that was outside of your comfort zone? I believe there is much more to being Spirit-filled than the Pentecostal experience of speaking in tongues. In fact, we are commanded to be filled with the Holy Spirit in Ephesians 5:18: "And be not drunk with wine, wherein is excess; but be filled with the Spirit" (KJV). The Greek word used for *filled* in that passage is *plēroō*, which means to make full, to fill up, to fill to the full, to cause to abound. We are commanded to be so "full" of the Holy Spirit that His presence and power are literally pouring out of us. As we follow the leading of the Holy Spirit, He will guide us into a life of the miraculous.

As I said before, I challenge you to allow the Holy Spirit to take you beyond your comfort zone. Do something you have never done before, in order to experience what you have never experienced before. If you are thinking that God would never lead you to do something that is uncomfortable, you have probably never read (or properly comprehended) the Bible.

Becoming a "Water Walker"

One of my favorite gospel accounts is the story of Peter walking on the water. It is almost beyond human comprehension, yet it absolutely happened. How? Well, first of all, before we talk about Peter walking on water, we must pay attention to the fact that Jesus walked on the water first. This is not really an account of Peter walking on water, but it is really an account of Peter following Jesus. "About three o'clock in the morning Jesus came toward them, walking on the water" (Matthew 14:25 NLT).

This is a very important detail that is often left out when people mention this story in the Bible. Jesus wasn't in the boat. Jesus wasn't on the shore. He was on the water. It would be one thing for the disciples to come to Jesus and ask Him, "Master, can we go and walk on the water?" But in reality, the disciples saw Jesus in a way that they had never witnessed Him before, and their first response was fear and anxiety. But Peter made a very profound request. "Then Peter called to him, 'Lord, if it's really you, tell me to come to you, walking on the water'" (verse 28 NLT). In other words, "Jesus, if this is who You really are, I want to follow You. I want to be with You where You are, even if it means walking on water to get there." To this request, Jesus replied, "Yes, come" (verse 29 NLT).

First, if you are going to operate in the supernatural, you must be willing to see Jesus in a way you have never seen Him before. He is so much more than you have realized. Second, the secret to the supernatural in this instance is the willingness to yield to Him no matter what. Peter wasn't simply walking on water—he was responding to an invitation by Jesus to step into the supernatural. If we step out of the boat and stand on His Word, we will find ourselves walking on water (i.e., operating in the miraculous power of God).

SUMMARY QUESTIONS

1. Why is God's design plan for ministering miracles important?
2. What are the characteristics of the spiritual blueprint of heaven?
3. Why is compassion the key to releasing miracles?
4. If we want to operate in the supernatural, what has to change?

MIRACLE ACTIVATION

Father, in the name of Jesus, I thank You that You have given me the divine blueprint for miracles. Thank You that the blood of Jesus grants me access to the supernatural power and presence of God. Now that I have access through Jesus, I declare that miracles are a frequent expression of Your presence in my life. I declare that I walk in Christlike compassion, and as a result I experience Your heart for the people around me. I declare that I am a "Water Walker" because I take bold risks in faith in order to experience the manifestation of Your power. In the name of Jesus, I declare that my life is conducive to the flow of Your miraculous power. Amen.

3

Understanding Biblical Faith

There's No Manifestation without the Manifester

For by grace you have been saved through faith, and that not of
yourselves; it is the gift of God.

Ephesians 2:8

Throughout this book we have talked about keys to walking in the supernatural power of God, primarily the importance of faith. As we continue to explore this topic,
I want us to establish a foundation for what biblical faith is and
why it is so necessary.

The book of Hebrews tells us, "Now faith is the substance of
things hoped for, the evidence of things not seen" (11:1). This
is a very powerful statement. We said before that the word *faith*
here comes from the Greek word *pistis*, which means confidence
or conviction. When we are operating in biblical faith, we have
an assurance that God is exactly who He says He is and that He

can do exactly what He says He can do. In verse 6, the writer of Hebrews put it this way: "But without faith it is impossible to please him: for he that cometh to God must believe that he is, and that he is a rewarder of them that diligently seek him" (KJV).

Faith is absolutely necessary in order to please God. We must believe that He is who He says, and that He rewards those who seek Him. What does this have to do with walking in miracles? Everything! It is through faith that we tap into the divine ability of God. Faith is not about getting God to do something—it is about believing and receiving what He has already done. The miraculous already belongs to the believer through divine inheritance, based upon what Jesus did on the cross. The *dynamis* power of God is already working in us via the Holy Spirit, but we place a demand on that power by faith.

What Is Biblical Faith?

The writer of Hebrews says that faith is the "substance." This is the Greek word *hupostasis*; it literally means support or "a standing under." In short, faith is the support system of spiritual life. It is the basis of your confidence and trust in God. Through faith we can be assured that what God says in His Word is absolutely true and that His promises shall surely come to pass. Faith is who we know God to be now, and hope is what we expect from God in the future. For example, the Bible says in Romans 10:17, "So then faith comes by hearing, and hearing by the word of God."

The first time we heard the Gospel, we received the revelation that Jesus was a real person and that He literally came in the flesh, died on a cross and was raised from the dead (see 1 Corinthians 15:1–4). We never saw Jesus physically. We were not alive two thousand years ago. How could we believe such a thing? Faith! As a result of that supernatural revelation, we were confident enough to confess Jesus as our Lord and believe that He could save us, and that we would go to heaven someday. As the old hymn goes, because He lives, we can face tomorrow.[1] This is what scholars would call "saving faith," but faith as a spiritual principle works the same way in every area of our lives. The same way we received salvation by faith is the same way we receive healing. The same way we receive healing is the same way we receive financial provision: hearing.

What we hear about God determines what we believe about God.

What we hear about God determines what we believe about God.

Faith versus Presumption

There is a very stark difference between biblical faith and presumption. Paul told us in Romans 10 that "faith comes by hearing." He goes on to say, "How then shall they call on Him in whom they have not believed?" (verse 14). We stated before that faith is our confidence or trust in God. You can only trust someone when you know their character. That character and integrity of the person assure you that they will do exactly what they say. This is not to be conflated with presumption. The *Oxford Dictionary* defines *presumption* as "an idea that is taken to be true, and often used as the basis for other ideas, although it is not known for certain." Presumption lacks certainty. It is hoping for the best without a basis for that hope.

Years ago, I remember a very traumatic experience. My wife and I were newly married. We didn't have an income at the time, but I convinced my wife that we should finance a new vehicle. As you can imagine, because we did not have an income, the car loan defaulted and we were in the process of going through a bank repossession. I can vividly remember praying and asking God to intervene and give us the money for the car. Well, the money never came. Actually, I thought that the car was caught up in the rapture, because it disappeared like a thief in the night. I was very frustrated and disappointed, but I learned a valuable lesson during that season: Faith is not the presumption that anything you want will happen. In fact, I remember God speaking to me. *I never told you to finance that car! That had nothing to do with Me!*

I was shocked. In other words, I was trying to force God to intervene in something He never authorized. Please don't get me wrong. I believe that God honors our faith and that He is merciful to intervene in situations that we find ourselves in through our own impatience and disobedience, but every wish and desire is not a genuine expression of biblical faith. The good news is that the very next day we were given a car debt-free. Hallelujah! God taught me how to live by genuine biblical faith.

Many people mistake faith for magic. They believe that if they say the magic words, then "voilà!" everything will materialize. Friends, that is not God's idea of faith at all.

Faith Operates within God's Will

There is a very important concept that you must grasp if you really desire to operate in biblical faith and walk in the supernatural power of God: Faith only operates where the will of God is known and acted upon. Earlier, we referenced Romans 10:10–14. No one can believe something of which they have no knowledge. Remember, confidence and trust are based upon your knowledge of the person in whom that trust is placed. It is reminiscent of a credit score. One of the reasons that financial institutions check a credit score is to evaluate a person's past financial behavior. Why? What you have done in the past is often an accurate measure of what you will do in the future (there are exceptions to this rule, of course).

The Bible says, "Therefore know that the LORD your God, He is God, the faithful God who keeps covenant and mercy for a thousand generations with those who love Him and keep His commandments" (Deuteronomy 7:9). God has always kept His word in the past. We can, therefore, confidently trust that He will be faithful to His word today. God has perfect credit. He has always met His obligations. The Bible goes on to say, "For ever, O Lord, thy word is settled in heaven" (Psalm 119:89 KJV). The psalmist uses an interesting Hebrew word, *nāṣaḇ*, which is translated "settled." It means to stand firm. In other words, the Word of God is a firm foundation. His Word is unshakable. His Word is eternal. God's Word is His will.

When we are convinced about the Word of God, we are convinced about the will of God. Where the will of God is known is the place where faith has its full efficacy. For example, why do we have the right to believe that God will physically heal us? Because physical healing is a promise from the Word of God. If we are ignorant of this promise, we will not have the confidence to believe God in that area of our lives. When I was struggling with sickness, I studied literally everything the Bible said about healing. By doing this I was gaining knowledge of what God's will was concerning healing. It is hard to have faith for something God never promised you. We know that Jesus is the Messiah, because He says He is. We have a guarantee. There is no guarantee where there is no promise.

Counterfeits of Biblical Faith

I can remember an interesting experience years ago. I was traveling through the airport, and I stopped by the shoe parlor to shine my shoes. As I waited for the attendant to work on my shoes, I noticed a man sitting next to me who was also getting his shoes polished. He was dressed in a nice business suit. He looked very successful. I also noticed that he was wearing a newer-model Rolex watch. I said to him, "Sir, that is a very nice watch you are wearing!" He replied, "Thank you so much! But it's not real!" I was shocked. He later told me that he paid $75 for the watch on his trip to China. He even took the watch off to let me examine it. I

41

am a fan of watches, so I knew exactly how an authentic Rolex is supposed to look and feel. But this apparent $20,000 Rolex was nothing more than a cheap counterfeit.

Just like my story about the watch, there are many counterfeits to biblical faith. I will highlight several of these counterfeits below and tell you why they are so dangerous. I will also draw a contrast between the genuine and the counterfeit.

Positive Thinking versus Biblical Faith

Years ago, I was watching a television program of a popular motivational speaker on the topic of positive confession and visualization. He talked about how we could visualize whatever we want and speak it into existence. He almost sounded like a Christian televangelist, but there was no mention of God or Jesus. Instead he referenced "the Universe." I immediately knew that this was not of God. Why? Faith is not about having what we want; biblical faith is about having what He wants. Does God grant us the desires of our heart? Absolutely! Does God grant us our desires? Yes! But those desires are not a manifestation from "the Universe." They are a gift from our omnibenevolent God. Biblical confession is not simply saying what we want, but it is from the Greek word *homologeo*, which means to say the same thing as another. In other words, we must say what God says. New Age positive confession focuses on self; biblical confession focuses on Christ. Many Christians have unknowingly opened themselves to the occult by engaging in New Age practices. Worse still is the mixture of these things into the Church.

The Bible says, "If you abide in Me, and My words abide in you, you will ask what you desire, and it shall be done for you" (John 15:7). We are told to ask for what we desire, but that asking comes from a posture of abiding in Christ (the Word of God) and acknowledging that our full reliance is on Him and not ourselves. We are called to abide in Him, believe His Word and obey His voice, and as a result, His power and presence flow through us.

We ask Him in faith, and He is the One who brings it to pass. We can ask for what we want because we abide in Him, and His words abide in us. The Bible says that we have the mind of Christ (see 1 Corinthians 2:16). Our provision does not come from "the Universe." Our provision and blessings—"every good gift and every perfect gift"—come from God, the authentic source of all good things, "the Father of lights, with whom there is no variation or shadow of turning" (James 1:17).

New Age Meditation versus Biblical Meditation

If you pay very close attention, you will notice that the word *meditation* has become a very popular buzzword. With the prevalence of Far Eastern practices like Buddhism, Taoism or Daoism, many people have embraced ideologies about meditation that are not biblical. First, I want to define meditation in general terms. In general, meditation means to think deeply or focus one's mind for a period of time, in silence or with the aid of chanting, for religious or spiritual purposes or as a method of relaxation. There are different forms of meditation, such as mindfulness meditation (i.e., slowing down your thoughts, observing your thinking). This meditation comes from the Eastern spiritual practices focused on emptying your mind, observing your thoughts and relaxing your body. The goal is to detach yourself from the present reality and transcend to a higher plain of thought.

This has nothing to do with biblical meditation. The Bible says, "This Book of the Law shall not depart from your mouth, but you shall meditate in it day and night, that you may observe to do according to all that is written in it. For then you will make your way prosperous, and then you will have good success" (Joshua 1:8). The word *meditate* here comes from the Hebrew word *hāgâ* (pronounced haw-gaw). This word means to moan, growl, utter, muse, mutter, meditate, devise, plot, speak. In short, it is the practice of speaking or muttering the Word of God over and over again. The ancient Israelites would speak the Torah under their breath with the goal of inculcating God's Word into their hearts. This is what the Scripture means by meditating on the Word.

In the New Testament we are told,

> Finally, brethren, whatever things are true, whatever things are noble, whatever things are just, whatever things are pure, whatever things are lovely, whatever things are of good report, if there is any virtue and if there is anything praiseworthy—meditate on these things.
>
> Philippians 4:8

We are to ponder on the promises of God daily. We are told to set our affections on things above. What does this have to do with miracles? We should meditate on God's Word in the areas where we desire to see a greater expression of His presence and power. Study the book of Acts and think about what God did in the early Church. Write down Scriptures on an index card and commit them to memory. Speak these Scriptures daily. This is an example of biblical meditation. New Age meditation is about emptying your mind; biblical meditation is about filling your mouth and spirit with the Word of God. New Age meditation can lead to demonization; biblical meditation leads to deliverance. Glory to God!

How to Build and Fortify Miraculous Faith

Jesus gives a powerful parable in the gospels that bears repeating. In Matthew 7:24–27, Jesus said,

> "Therefore whoever hears these sayings of Mine, and does them, I will liken him to a wise man who built his house on the rock: and the rain descended, the floods came, and the winds blew and beat on that house; and it did not fall, for it was founded on the rock.
>
> "But everyone who hears these sayings of Mine, and does not do them, will be like a foolish man who built his house on the sand: and the rain descended, the floods came, and the winds blew and beat on that house; and it fell. And great was its fall."

We looked at this parable in an earlier chapter, but I want to reemphasize this biblical truth because of its importance. Being a hearer and doer of the Word of God is critical to developing biblical faith. God's Word is the foundation of supernatural living. You will never operate in the miraculous consistently until you learn to both hear and do what God says. Earlier, I referenced Romans 10:17 ("faith comes by hearing"). This is very critical. What does the Word of God say? What do you hear the Word of God say? Have you acted upon what you heard? These are critical questions in developing a supernatural lifestyle. Ask yourself, Is my faith rooted in the Word of God?

The writer of Hebrews tells us that we should look to Jesus as the "author and finisher of our faith" (Hebrews 12:2). Our faith starts and ends with Jesus. He is the Source. He is the "chief cornerstone" (Ephesians 2:20). Not only must we have a solid knowledge of the Word of God, but we must respond to the Word of God with corresponding actions. James said, "But be doers of the word, and not hearers only, deceiving yourselves" (James 1:22). He also said, "Faith without works is dead" (2:20).

Here are some practical steps:

1. Study and meditate on the Word of God.
2. Ask God to speak to you through His Word.
3. Release your faith for what He has promised.
4. Act on the directives and promptings of the Holy Spirit.
5. Thank Him for the manifestation of His Word.
6. Repeat.

Getting to Know the Manifester

Years ago, God gave me a simple task: *You do the believing, I will do the manifesting.* As simple as this statement was, it was very powerful. I realized at that moment that "manifesting" was not my responsibility. This is another term that has been hijacked by the

New Age community. In their definition, this means to cause what you want to materialize, but that is not how I am using the term at all. When I talk about manifesting, I am talking about something moving from an unseen expectation to a visible demonstration. It is to show the evidence or proof of something. Living a supernatural life is not about "manifesting"—it is about getting to know the "Manifester." Jesus is the "Manifester." He is the One who brings things to pass.

> **Living a supernatural life is not about "manifesting"—it is about getting to know the "Manifester."**

Seeing miracles is not about squinting your eyes really hard until something appears. Miracles are about intimacy with the one who is omnipotent. As we plug our faith into His Word (which is the true power source), we will see the manifestation of His miraculous power. Remember, the purpose of the miraculous is to bring glory to God. Apart from Him we can "do nothing" (John 15:5).

I can remember praying to God one day and asking Him for more of His power. The Lord didn't say a word. Then all of a sudden, I heard His still, small voice say, *Move out of My way!* I got the picture very quickly. The truth is, God doesn't need our help. He simply wants us to believe and trust Him. I am reminded of a statement the late John Wimber made. He essentially said that he was not arrogant if someone got healed in his meetings and neither was he broken if someone didn't get healed, because it was God's job, not his.

If we will simply believe, we will see the glory of God.

SUMMARY QUESTIONS

1. What is the difference between faith and hope?
2. What are some counterfeits to biblical faith?

3. What are the differences between New Age meditation and biblical meditation?

4. What are practical steps to meditating on the Word?

MIRACLE ACTIVATION

Father, in the name of Jesus, I thank You for who You are and all that You have done in my life. I thank You that You have given me supernatural faith to believe and trust in Your Word. I declare that I have miraculous, mountain-moving faith. I declare that I have an experiential knowledge of God and His will; therefore, I have the faith to experience miracles daily. As I release my faith now, according to the Word of God, something supernatural is happening in and through my life for the glory of God. Thank You, Lord, for miraculous breakthroughs in my life in the name of Jesus. Amen!

4

Personal Revival

The Power of Consecration

"But you, when you pray, go into your room, and when you have shut your door, pray to your Father who is in the secret place; and your Father who sees in secret will reward you openly."

Matthew 6:6

Many years ago, I attended a church service that a friend of mine invited me to. I vividly remember that it was in the evening, and when we walked into the building, I could hear strange music (at least it was strange to me at the time). I was a brand-new believer, and I knew nothing of the supernatural, except the time when I heard the audible voice of God calling me into the ministry (a story I will save for another time). As we sat down in the sanctuary, the preacher was wearing a white suit, and there were deacons and elders standing in front of him on both sides; it looked like a *Soul Train* line. I was waiting for Don

Cornelius to come out from the back of the church. As I continued to stare at the preacher, I noticed that he would call people up for prayer and they would fall to the ground as he touched them.

I thought, *This is crazy! How could they let him knock them out like that? All they have to do is tighten their knees!* Then I thought, *He would never knock me out like that!* As I looked up, the preacher was staring at me, and suddenly, he told the ushers to bring me near the altar. I obliged his request out of respect. As I was walking toward the preacher, a fleeting thought passed through my mind: *I am not falling down!* Ironically, I fell to the ground before I ever reached him, and the ushers had to drag me back to my seat. I was so embarrassed.

There was something odd about the experience—odd in a very good way. I literally felt the presence of God. It felt as if God's love wrapped around me like liquid love. My life was never the same after that experience.

Intimacy: Living in the Secret Place

The story I shared with you earlier is not just a story of a strange experience that I had as a young believer, but it is indeed a story of personal revival. Every time we have a personal supernatural encounter with God, we are awakened to a greater reality of who He is. That is exactly what happened to me, and I believe this is exactly what will happen to you as you read this book and act on things that are shared. I realized from that experience that one of the keys to being able to experience the supernatural consistently, and walk in the power of God in a way that impacts others, is intimacy. God wants to know us and be known by us. He wants us to experience deep communion and fellowship with His Spirit.

Jesus said, "But you, when you pray, go into your room, and when you have shut your door, pray to your Father who is in the secret place; and your Father who sees in secret will reward you openly" (Matthew 6:6). Here He was telling His disciples that when they pray, they should go into their "room" and shut the door and pray to the Father "who is in the secret place." What is the secret place? Jesus uses the idiomatic expressions "closet" (KJV) and "secret place" in this verse intentionally. This is a reference to the bedchamber that a husband and wife enter in order to consummate their marital union. In other words, when a couple married in the ancient world, they would go into a tent or bedchamber, and they would be intimate. This was a covenant act of love and devotion. The goal was not only to consummate the union but to conceive a child. This is exactly what our Lord says in Matthew 6:6. We are to go into the place of intimacy with God until we conceive and eventually birth the miraculous.

I know I may have lost several of you with this concept, but trust me, it is absolutely scriptural. The word *secret* here comes from the Greek word *kryptos*, which means hidden or concealed. We must understand that God hides things for us, not *from* us. This is why the book of Hebrews says, "But without faith it is impossible to please Him, for he who comes to God must believe that He is, and that He is a rewarder of those who diligently seek Him" (11:6).

Intimacy is a passionate pursuit to discover something about someone that is not known or seen by everyone else. A husband can see things about his wife that others are not privy to. Why? Because he has a covenant relationship with her that grants him access to the secret things about her. These things are hidden from him during the courtship process, but they are revealed to him as he continues to seek a deeper relationship with her, culminating in physical and emotional intimacy within marriage. To dwell in the secret place, therefore, is to dwell in the place of spiritual intimacy and communion with God.

The Power of Consecration

There is something I discovered about God that is absolutely vital in walking in the supernatural. The more set apart we are, the greater the manifestation of His presence and power in and through us. We live in an age when Christianity has become extremely post-modern in many ways. By Christianity, I am specifically referring to American or Western Church culture. There is a push for the whole "less is more" concept. Our church services have become much shorter, and in some cases less demanding and less impact-ful. We are seeing an integration of popular culture with modern Christianity. This has led to an emergent church that looks very much like the world.

The Bible says this: "But as He who called you is holy, you also be holy in all your conduct" (1 Peter 1:15). The word *holy* here comes from the Greek word *hagios*, which means sacred, pure, blameless or consecrated. Simply put, to be holy is to be consecrated or set apart for God's pleasure and His divine purpose. If we are going to experience personal revival, we must embrace a life of purity. The greater the purity, the greater the power. Please make no mistake: Holiness is the direct consequence of what Jesus accomplished on the cross and not what we are able to do in our own strength. We are made holy by the blood of the Lamb, Jesus. We must, however, appropriate that holiness in our daily lives by separating ourselves from unclean things as we are empowered by the Holy Spirit.

Have you ever read a label that said "100 percent pure"? This means that whatever you are consuming has not been diluted with water or other fillers. Usually, things that are 100 percent pure have a stronger flavor or effect than things that are not pure. The same is true of our spiritual lives. The more purity we embrace, the more potent our spiritual lives will be. This is not an old-fashioned concept but a necessity for victorious living.

Developing a Miracle Mindset

Years ago, I didn't understand the concept of the supernatural. I considered myself a consummate intellectual. If I couldn't wrap my mind around something, I would simply dismiss it as illogical.

It is almost embarrassing to think about how proud and critical I was at that time. Thank God for His mercy and lovingkindness. Many people today are locked into a mindset of spiritual limitation. To them, God is only as big as their denomination or theological framework. One person told me that the Baptist church was the first church in the Bible. When I asked about the basis for this theory, the response I got was, "John was a Baptist! The Bible called him John the Baptist!" As funny as this statement may seem, I can assure that they were not joking at all. You may not have come from the Baptist church, but all of us are greatly influenced by our religious upbringing, whether it was Episcopalian, Catholic, nondenominational, atheist or American heathen.

The Bible tells us that "the carnal mind is enmity against God; for it is not subject to the law of God" (Romans 8:7). This means that if we are to live a supernatural lifestyle, we must change the way we think. We cannot possess a carnal mentality (a mindset that is primarily focused on natural things). We must develop a miracle mindset. What is a miracle mindset? A miracle mindset is a mentality that embraces the miraculous as a normal way of life. It is a mindset that doesn't just focus on the things it can see only.

The Bible says, "While we look not at the things which are seen, but at the things which are not seen: for the things which are seen are temporal; but the things which are not seen are eternal" (2 Corinthians 4:18). Are you facing challenges today? Are there natural limitations that you find difficult to overcome? It's time to change your perspective. It is time for you to think differently. "And do not be conformed to this world, but be transformed by the renewing of your mind, that you may prove what is that good and acceptable and perfect will of God" (Romans 12:2).

Cultivating a Miraculous Culture

Years ago, I went to Africa for the first time in my life. I will never forget this experience. I can vividly remember arriving at the airport in Lagos, Nigeria, and deboarding the plane. As soon as we retrieved our baggage and went outside the terminal, I immediately knew that I was not in Kansas anymore. People spoke Yoruba. Taxi drivers fought for customers. But that could be seen in New York City or Houston, Texas. The part that really perplexed me was when we arrived at the house of our host, the servants bowed before me. It was like a scene from a movie. I quickly understood that this was not only a different country, but it was a totally different culture. The truth is, the only thing that really separates people (besides religion and politics) is culture and language. *Culture* is defined as "the customs, arts, social institutions, and achievements of a particular nation, people, or other social group." I like to define *culture* as the commonly accepted way of doing things of a particular country or group.

In Matthew 6:33, Jesus said, "But seek first the kingdom of God and His righteousness, and all these things shall be added to you." The word *righteousness* here comes from the Greek word *dikaiosynē*, which means, among other things, correctness of thinking. The Bible is literally telling us that we must seek God's Kingdom and the right way of thinking, and as a result, "all these things will be added to you." Glory to God! You mean to tell me that the way I think matters? Absolutely! We must embrace Kingdom culture if we want to live a life of the supernatural.

Again, this is why it is a requirement to renew your mind. What ways of thinking that you currently embrace need to change? Maybe you need to change the way you think about prayer. Maybe you need to change the way you think about miracles. The moment your thinking begins to change is the moment your life begins to change. We must imbibe a culture of the supernatural. Just as we must embrace the language and the customs when we travel to a different country, we, too, must adjust our spiritual mindset to position ourselves to experience and walk in all that God has made available to us. Once we imbibe the culture of the Kingdom of God, we must develop that culture around us. And it is important to understand that at the foundation of miracles is a culture of love.

Stop Waiting for Revival

Contrary to popular opinion, revival is not coming "someday," whenever God decides to get off His heavenly rocking chair and move on the earth. The greatest revival in human history began two thousand years ago. We are not waiting on God to move. There is no need to wait for revival—what part do we play as believers to step into these realities? The reason I ask what part we play is due to the fact that we must understand our personal role in God's plan to pour out His glory and power through us.

One of the most debilitating things in the Church right now is an overemphasis on the hyper-sovereignty of God. What do I mean by this? There is this belief that God moves independently from us. This statement is partially true, but incomplete. Don't get me wrong, God is definitely omnipotent, but He desires our active participation in what He does in and through us. I like to put it this way: Revival takes place when revived people take action. If we are the hands and feet of Jesus, then how many people does Jesus touch through us in a given day? How many sick people are healed? How many blind eyes are opened? Don't wait to hear an ominous voice or for the heavens to literally open above you. Heaven is already opened, and God has already spoken.

> **Revival takes place when revived people take action.**

Jesus said, "Go into all the world and preach the gospel to every creature" (Mark 16:15). This is not about performing some religious activity that gives us points with God; this is about stepping into a spiritual reality that has already been established and commissioned by Jesus. A world where anything is possible according to God's Word. Think about what I just said: God wants us to live in a different reality from what we have been accustomed to. A reality where church starts the minute we open our eyes. A reality marked by constant communion with God, where we see from His perspective and act on the promptings of the Holy Spirit to see lives transformed for the glory of God. A reality where worship is a lifestyle, not just a sequence of songs.

New Mentality—New Reality

Earlier, we talked about developing a miracle mindset. I believe that the renewing of our mind is a vital component to living a supernatural life. We must intentionally challenge and change our mentality. What do I mean by this statement? We mentioned this concept earlier, but it bears repeating. We must first define what a mentality is. A mentality is the characteristic attitude of mind or way of thinking of a person or group. We all have a way of thinking that has been deeply influenced by our environment and/or culture. The key is to make sure that the way we think aligns with the Word of God, and if it doesn't, we must change our thinking, or in some cases demolish it altogether. This is what Paul was referring to in 2 Corinthians 10:4–5 (KJV):

> For the weapons of our warfare are not carnal, but mighty through God to the pulling down of strong holds; casting down imaginations, and every high thing that exalteth itself against the knowledge of God, and bringing into captivity every thought to the obedience of Christ.

The apostle Paul, in his second epistle to the Corinthian church, told us that we must "cast down imaginations." What does this actually mean? First, the word *imaginations* here comes from the Greek word *logismos*, which means reasonings or arguments. These are ways of thinking that are hostile to the Word of God. The Bible refers to these thought patterns in the same verse as "strong holds" or residential fortresses that hinder the purposes of God in our lives. These fortresses must be demolished by the truth. What is the truth? The truth is the Gospel. The truth is that you and I are unconditionally loved by our heavenly Father. The truth is, we were born for miracles. It is part and parcel with our born-again spiritual DNA.

God's Love—Foundation of the Miraculous

If we are going to build a new mentality, we must make sure that we are building upon the right foundation. We have said before that miracles are an expression of the love of God. I would go further to say that an understanding of the love of God is the foundation for the miraculous. The Bible says, "For in Christ Jesus neither circumcision nor uncircumcision avails anything, but faith working through love" (Galatians 5:6). The ethos of our faith in God or the manifestation of His supernatural power is the love of God.

I stated in chapter 1 that the Gospel is indeed a love story—God's love for humanity confirmed in the incarnation, death, burial and resurrection of Jesus. It was the single greatest act of love in the history of the cosmos. The Bible says, "For God so loved the world, that he gave his only begotten Son, that whosoever believeth in him should not perish, but have everlasting life" (John 3:16 KJV). Everything that God does for us is a consequence of His love. The same is true of the miraculous. The culture of miracles is based upon the revelation of the omnibenevolent love of God. We don't minister healing to the sick to prove that we are super-spiritual. We minister in the supernatural to demonstrate that God loves people. He loves people so much, He is willing to intervene in their affairs.

God loves you. He desires to manifest His love through you. Love is not self-seeking or self-centered. We must be assured that God loves us if we are to walk in the confidence necessary to operate in miracles. Despite your past failures or current limitations, you qualify as a vessel through whom God can display His glorious power. Isn't that good news?

SUMMARY QUESTIONS

1. What role does intimacy with God play in miracles?
2. Where is the "secret place" where you find God?
3. How do we cultivate an atmosphere conducive to miracles?
4. What is the relationship between the love of God and the miraculous?

MIRACLE ACTIVATION

Father, in the name of Jesus, I thank You for Your supernatural presence and power working in my life. I declare that I dwell in and operate from a place of deep intimacy and fellowship with Your Spirit. I declare that Your presence flows in and through my life for Your glory. I declare that I operate in the supernatural love of God, which enables me to operate in supernatural faith for miracles, signs and wonders. I declare that my thought process is lined up with Your Word; I think Your thoughts and fulfill Your desires. I declare that I live in a constant state of expectancy and faith, always looking for You to manifest Yourself in a fresh way. In Jesus' name, Amen.

5

Hearing God's Voice

The Source of Faith for Miracles

"My sheep hear My voice, and I know them, and they follow Me."

John 10:27

He squinted his eyes to avoid the agitation of the sand-filled air, while the dry desert atmosphere made him feel thirsty. He covered his face with a cloth as he led his father-in-law's sheep to the backside of the desert. The bleating of the sheep echoed as he reached the mountain called Horeb. As he gazed at the mountain, he saw something peculiar. A bush was burning, yet not consumed by the flame. This sight was so intriguing he felt compelled to turn aside and investigate this phenomenon more closely.

As he came closer to the bush, he heard a voice coming from it, saying, "Moses, Moses."

Moses said, "Here I am."

Then the voice said, "Do not draw near this place. Take your sandals off your feet, for the place where you stand is holy ground."

The account of Moses and the burning bush found in Exodus 3:1–5 is a profound story of a man who heard the voice of God and was forever changed by the voice he heard. I believe that hearing the voice of God is both possible and vital for every Christian today. I also believe that hearing God's voice is essential to walking in the supernatural power of God. Why? When we read the account of Moses found in Exodus, we see that his journey into the miraculous began with hearing and responding to the voice of God. As Moses looked more deeply into what he saw, God gave him instructions on how to lead His people out of bondage.

Remove Your Shoes

One of the most important parts of this story is also the most often overlooked. When Moses drew closer to the burning bush, God spoke to him and said, "Do not draw near this place. Take your sandals off your feet, for the place where you stand is holy ground" (Exodus 3:5). Why is this an important detail? The sandals in Scripture represent a person's vocation, path or way of life. In other words, God was telling Moses, *Before you come closer to Me, be willing to have a radical change in the way you walk.* If we want to hear God's voice, we must first remove our sandals and acknowledge that He is holy. We must revere His presence and His voice. This is a key spiritual principle in hearing God. We will never hear from the God we don't revere.

There are many people today who find it challenging and some who find it nearly impossible to hear the voice of God. What does God even sound like? While some are waiting for the voice of Charlton Heston to scream in their ears, others are waiting to see an actual burning bush. Regardless of which category you fall into, it is important for you to know beyond a shadow of a doubt that God speaks today. What does this have to do with miracles? Everything!

My Experience Hearing God's Audible Voice

Many years ago, I was coming back from a fishing trip in Florida with my dad. As a young kid, I often daydreamed, and this particular day was no different. I can vividly remember looking out the window and gazing at the sky when suddenly the clouds opened and I heard the audible voice of God. He said, "Preach My Word!" It was so authoritative and ominous that the voice literally resonated inside me. As I write these words, I can hear that same voice all over again. I absolutely knew that God was speaking to me. That was the first time I heard the audible voice of God and my calling into the ministry. That was not the last time I heard that voice. Since then, I have come to discover that God speaks to His children in many ways. As you read this chapter, my prayer for you is that you, too, will hear His voice clearly, and that you will be forever changed by the voice you hear.

Understanding the Ways God Speaks

Before we go deeper into the correlation between hearing the voice of God and walking in miracles, I want to take a few moments to identify and explain the various ways God speaks to us. Once you understand the ways God speaks to you, you will have an increased confidence to hear God's voice and respond accordingly. After all, your miracle, or the miracle God will use to impart to someone else through you, is one word away.

There are five main ways God speaks to human beings. This is not necessarily an exhaustive list, but it is a biblical synopsis.

1. God speaks through His Word.
2. God speaks through His servants.

3. God speaks through dreams and visions.

4. God speaks through the promptings of the Holy Spirit.

5. God speaks through circumstances.

I believe these are the ways He continues to speak to His children today.

Through His Word

The Bible says, "In the beginning was the Word, and the Word was with God, and the Word was God" (John 1:1). If we are to hear the voice of God and walk in the miraculous, we must understand that God primarily speaks through His written and revealed Word. God will not say anything to us that is not in harmony with His Word. Why? The Bible is clear: "And the Word was God." Simply put, God and His Word are one. The word for *Word* here is the Greek word *logos*, which means the living voice or a thought. The *logos* is that which gives form and purpose to everything in the universe, because everything in the known and unknown universe was created by the Word. That is very heavy, right? This is where we get the English word *theology* (*theos* and *logos*), which literally implies "what we say about God."

We must always make sure that what we say about God is what He says about Himself. The first key to hearing the voice of God, therefore, is reading, studying, meditating and knowing the Word. The more you read what God says, the more you will hear what God says.

Through His Servants

This may seem like an antiquated and archaic concept, but I am convinced that God still speaks through the men and women He has called and raised up for His purpose. The Bible says,

> "And I will give you shepherds according to My heart, who will feed you with knowledge and understanding. . . . I will set up shepherds

over them who will feed them; and they shall fear no more, nor be dismayed, nor shall they be lacking," says the LORD.

Jeremiah 3:15; 23:4

God promised in His Word that He would give us shepherds who would feed us with knowledge and understanding. We know that all knowledge and truth ultimately come from God, but God speaks through people. This can be through a sermon, seminar, book, video or conversation. Just as God spoke through the prophets of old, I believe that He is still speaking through His prophetic people today.

Through Dreams and Visions

Much of what we record in Scripture as a divine revelation from God came to the recipients of those revelations in the form of dreams and visions. God showed Jacob in a dream that He would make a covenant with him. God showed Joseph in a dream that he would be a ruler over Egypt. Isaiah saw a vision of the Lord seated on the throne. Ezekiel saw a vision of the wheel in the middle of the wheel. Peter had a vision of the sheet let down from heaven that prompted the outpouring of the Holy Spirit on the Gentiles. The list goes on and on. God promised to pour out His Spirit on all flesh. The Bible says,

> "And it shall come to pass afterward that I will pour out My Spirit on all flesh; your sons and your daughters shall prophesy, your old men shall dream dreams, your young men shall see visions."

Joel 2:28

I believe that God is still speaking today through dreams and visions. I believe that many people are receiving prophetic dreams and other supernatural encounters that God uses to communicate vital messages that can transform our lives. Again, we must use the Word as the ultimate litmus test to ensure that these dreams and visions indeed come from God.

Through the Promptings of the Holy Spirit

One of my favorite verses is found in the first epistle of the apostle John (2:27):

> But the anointing which you have received from Him abides in you, and you do not need that anyone teach you; but as the same anointing teaches you concerning all things, and is true, and is not a lie, and just as it has taught you, you will abide in Him.

John wrote to the early Church, addressing the false teachings of Gnosticism. This was essentially the belief and teaching that Jesus did not come in the flesh, but He was a spiritual being who came to enlighten humanity. They taught that the physical world was evil and the spiritual world was good. This teaching is also called Gnostic dualism. The apostle John tells the early Church that the anointing of the Holy Spirit is their Teacher. We are told in the gospel of John that the Holy Spirit will lead us into all truth. God, therefore, speaks to us through the promptings of the Holy Spirit. This is the inner nudging or knowing that we have that God is speaking to us about a specific thing. This can be a still, small voice or a strong impression on the inside of us. This unction of the Holy Spirit can come as a warning against deception or a strong inner witness to take a certain action (such as sharing our faith with a particular person). Either way, we must learn to pay close attention to God's promptings.

Through Circumstances

Another way that God speaks to us is through circumstances. One of the classic examples of this is found in Genesis 24:27: "And he said, 'Blessed be the LORD God of my master Abraham, who has not forsaken His mercy and His truth toward my master. As for me, being on the way, the LORD led me to the house of my master's brethren.'" When Abraham sent his servant to find a wife for his son Isaac, he gave the servant very specific instructions not to choose a wife from among the Canaanite women. The servant prayed,

"O LORD God of my master Abraham, please give me success this day, and show kindness to my master Abraham. Behold, here I stand by the well of water, and the daughters of the men of the city are coming out to draw water. Now let it be that the young woman to whom I say, 'Please let down your pitcher that I may drink,' and she says, 'Drink, and I will also give your camels a drink'—let her be the one You have appointed for Your servant Isaac. And by this I will know that You have shown kindness to my master."

And it happened, before he had finished speaking, that behold, Rebekah, who was born to Bethuel, son of Milcah, the wife of Nahor, Abraham's brother, came out with her pitcher on her shoulder.

verses 12–15

God answered the servant's prayer via circumstances. Many times God will order our steps or cause us to come into the path He has foreordained for us to walk in. This is why we must pay attention to the things that transpire in our daily lives. We must be as sons of Isaachar, discerning the times and the seasons. Sometimes, it is as simple as focusing on the things that take place around us and acknowledging that God is indeed confirming His word to us. Sometimes people ask God to "send a sign," and He does on many occasions. There are other times when God allows certain doors to close. In both cases, God is speaking. Are you listening?

"My Sheep Hear My Voice"

Jesus made a profound statement in the gospel of John: "My sheep hear My voice, and I know them, and they follow Me" (10:27). What does this mean?

Years ago, I was in a class where the professor was recounting one of his trips to Israel. He said there was a particular town that they traveled to where there were hundreds of sheep grazing in the same pasture. He was focused on a particular shepherd who stood up and walked away while blowing a silent whistle. Only his sheep stood and followed him while the other sheep remained.

This was a perfect illustration of the words Jesus spoke: "My sheep hear My voice." We must become acclimated to the voice of God. Just as the sheep could hear the whistle that the shepherd blew, we must learn to clearly discern the voice of God. The connection between a shepherd and his sheep is relational. The sheep develop a connection with their shepherd that allows them to hear the shepherd's voice amid the noise. His voice is distinct from all other shepherds.

If we are going to walk in the miraculous power and presence of God, we, too, must become deeply connected with the voice of the Good Shepherd. We must learn to hear and properly respond to the voice of God. How can we believe the voice we have not learned to identify?

Hearing First, Then Faith

Earlier, I mentioned how critical hearing the voice of God is to supernatural living. In fact, what we hear determines what we believe. Once we hear the voice of God, then we have the faith to believe God for the impossible. Contrary to popular belief, faith is not just some metaphysical force that you conjure with a magic wand. It is not the result of our own determination. Faith is the byproduct of what we hear.

The Bible says in Romans 10:17, "So then faith comes by hearing, and hearing by the word of God." The word *faith* comes from the Greek word *pistis*, which means confidence or conviction. Faith is the conviction of the truth, authority and power of the Word of God. The reason we can believe and trust God is because He has revealed Himself as reliable and trustworthy through His Word. This is why you cannot exercise biblical faith where the will of God is unknown.

Why do I have faith to operate in miracles today? Because God commanded us to preach the Word and He promised that signs and wonders would follow those who believe (see Mark 16:17). I believe! Signs and wonders, therefore, follow me. If God says it, then that settles it. Right? Not necessarily. Many people take things in the Bible out of context. For example, they read "Forever, O LORD, Your word is settled in heaven" (Psalm 119:89) to mean that if God's Word is settled in heaven, then it will automatically happen on earth. Friends, God's Word is settled in heaven, but faith is required for the Word of God to be settled in your heart.

The Bible says, "Now faith is the substance of things hoped for, the evidence of things not seen" (Hebrews 11:1). The word *substance* here comes from the Greek word *hypostasis*, which means a "setting or placing under," or "thing put under, substructure, foundation." One way to say it is that faith is the "firm foundation" upon which the believer's confident expectation in God is built. Yes! We can have a confident expectation of the future because of our faith in God. In other words, when God reveals Himself to us (through the written or spoken word), we can have confidence in who He reveals Himself to be. Because God says He is the Healer, we can have faith for healing. Because God says we can operate in miracles, I can have faith for the miraculous power of God. Faith is indeed the foundation of our spiritual lives. The writer of Hebrews went on to say, "But without faith it is impossible to please Him, for he who comes to God must believe that He is, and that He is a rewarder of those who diligently seek Him" (verse 6).

If you desire to experience God on a deeper level and operate in His supernatural power, you must learn to walk in biblical faith. I often tell people: Faith is not about getting God to do something. Faith is about believing and receiving what He has already done. The myth in the charismatic world is that one must be really deep and spiritual to operate in miracles, when the truth is that one must only believe by faith that God is exactly who He says He is. We often hear expressions like "Faith moves God." I have no doubt that there is truth to this statement, but what I have discovered in my many years as a Christian is that *faith moves us.* The moment we believe God by faith is the moment we move from information to revelation to manifestation and come into perfect alignment with His divine purposes.

> **Faith is not about getting God to do something. Faith is about believing and receiving what He has already done.**

Hearing Imparts Faith for Miracles

Hearing God's voice imparts faith for miracles. So the question remains, How does one attain the level of faith or spirituality necessary to operate in miracles? You don't! Faith is not attained; it is received.

The Bible says this in Galatians 3:5: "Therefore He who supplies the Spirit to you and works miracles among you, does He do it by the works of the law, or by the hearing of faith?" The apostle Paul established in his epistle to the churches in the Galatian province that miracles were not the result of the law, but miracles were the result of what he calls "the hearing of faith." He used the Greek word *akoē*, which means the sense of hearing or the organ of hearing. Simply put, those who see the manifestation of miracles are those who have exercised their spiritual ears to hear. The issue here is not simply believing more or having more faith, but the real key is hearing clearly.

Years ago, I was ministering at the Healing School in Tampa, and I invited people who were battling sickness to come to the front for prayer. A few people came forward, but no one was healed. I asked God why no one was being healed, and I heard a still, small voice say, *You are praying for the wrong thing!* So I asked the Holy Spirit what I should be focused on, and I heard Him say, *Bitterness, resentment and unforgiveness.* Immediately, I received illumination and faith to do exactly what God spoke to me. I asked the congregation to come forward for prayer if they were struggling with bitterness, resentment or unforgiveness. As I lifted my eyes, the altar was absolutely full. I then proceeded to lead people in a prayer of repentance and renunciation. Hundreds began to weep as they asked God to forgive them for harboring toxic emotions. All of sudden, people were healed instantly. One woman who had fibromyalgia for twenty years was totally healed. Another woman who had rheumatoid arthritis was instantly healed. Yet another person who dealt with chronic pain for years was healed by the power of God. Glory to God! As I responded to the voice of God and released my faith, miracles were manifested.

Work Miracles by the Hearing of Faith

It is important for us to understand that miracles are not the result of self-effort or self-righteousness. They are the result of divine empowerment—the grace of God and faith in His Word. This was a theme very common in the book of Galatians. Why? The apostle Paul was addressing the false teachings of the Judaizers, who taught that justification came through adherence to the Law of Moses. Paul called this doctrine of legalism "any other gospel" in Galatians 1:8: "But even if we, or an angel from heaven, preach any other gospel to you than what we have preached to you, let him be accursed." Paul also referred to it as witchcraft. "O foolish Galatians! Who has bewitched you that you should not obey the truth, before whose eyes Jesus Christ was clearly portrayed among you as crucified?" (3:1).

Why does Paul use such strong language to address this false teaching? At the core of the Gospel is the grace and omnibenevolence of God, not the self-righteousness of man. Walking in the supernatural is no exception. We are able to operate in the gifts and power of God because of the divine empowerment of the Holy Spirit in us, not as a consequence of religious practices or rituals. God flows through us miraculously as we release our faith, not as we attempt to achieve results through human effort.

Why is this such an important distinction? Many well-meaning Christians are frustrated because they are trying to discover the formula for miracles. Some believe it's more followers on social media. Others believe it is a prime-time spot on Christian television, while still others believe that if they devote themselves to pious activities or attend more conferences they will discover the secret. The truth is that Jesus gave us the secret: "Most assuredly, I say to you, he who believes in Me, the works that I do he will do also; and greater works than these he will do, because I go to My Father" (John 14:12).

As mentioned earlier in the chapter, miracles are the result of the hearing of faith. Again, this is why we must learn to develop our spiritual ears so that we will be able to hear God clearly. Just as God gave me the divine instruction to pray for people struggling with bitterness, resentment and unforgiveness and it resulted in healing miracles, God wants you to hear the divine instruction that will result in you seeing the miraculous in your own life consistently. What has God been saying to you lately? Have you responded accordingly? What areas of your life require divine intervention? What has the Holy Spirit prompted you to do in those specific areas? Remember this, attached to every miracle is a divine instruction. If you want to see the miracle, you must hear and respond to the divine instruction.

Friends, I am here to tell you it is time to silence the voices of the "Judaizers" of our day who seek to convince people that faith isn't enough. If you will simply believe, "you will see the glory of God" (John 11:40 NIV).

Refining Our Spiritual Hearing

The Bible says, "How then shall they call on Him in whom they have not believed?" and that "faith comes by hearing, and hearing by the word of God" (Romans 10:14, 17). So the question remains, How can you believe in Him whom you have not heard? This is where most people have a serious challenge. We must make sure that our theology is correct. By *theology* I'm not referring to seminary or Bible school (though I encourage Christian education). Instead, I'm referring to the essence of the word *theology*, meaning what God says about Himself. As I have said before, we must ensure that what we know and believe about God is in alignment with who God says He is.

Why is this such an important factor? Because I will never have faith for what I have never heard. You had to hear the Gospel first before you could believe in salvation. You must hear that God is the Healer in order to have faith for healing. So if you sit in a church that teaches that God doesn't physically heal people today (which is absolutely ridiculous), you will find it difficult to have the bold confidence that you can believe God to heal you or minister healing through you. If you never study the Word of God to know what He says about Himself and about you, how will you be able to trust Him for the supernatural? The truth is, we serve a supernatural God. The more you spend time in His Word, the more clearly you will hear His voice, and the more clearly you hear His voice, the more supernatural faith you will operate in. And the more supernatural faith you operate in, the more miracles you will see. Hallelujah!

SUMMARY QUESTIONS

1. Why is God's voice essential in walking in the supernatural?
2. What are the ways in which God speaks?

3. How does God speak through our circumstances?
4. Why is it important to recognize that miracles come from the grace of God and faith in His Word—not from self-effort?

MIRACLE ACTIVATION

Father, in the name of Jesus, Your Word declares that Your sheep hear Your voice and they will not follow the voice of a stranger. I declare that I am Your sheep and that I hear Your voice. I will not follow the voice of a stranger. I declare that my spiritual ears are sensitive to Your voice and that I walk in consistent obedience to Your will. I declare that all "spiritual interference" is removed from my life and that I possess an acute ability to hear the Word of God. Anything that has been planted in my life that would hinder me from hearing and obeying the voice of God is uprooted in the name of Jesus.

6

Prayer

Our Spiritual Power Source

Confess your faults one to another, and pray one for another, that ye may be healed. The effectual fervent prayer of a righteous man availeth much.

James 5:16 KJV

His heart raced as he stood before the king of Israel. With every beat, he felt a greater boldness that overwhelmed his body. Armed with a mandate from God, he faced the most powerful man in Israel. With a straight face, he declared, "It will not rain in Israel for three years and six months." As he stood, he could sense a shift in the atmosphere as great dread fell upon the king and his court. From that day, there was not a drop of rain in Israel.

The Bible tells us that "Elijah was a man with a nature like ours, and he prayed earnestly that it would not rain; and it did not rain on the land for three years and six months" (James 5:17).

This is a profound example of the purpose and power of prayer. As believers, we must understand the critical nature of prayer and the mandate we have been given by God to pray without ceasing. What is prayer, and what does it have to do with supernatural living? I am glad you asked! The ancient art of prayer has been a timeless practice of inviting God to intervene in the affairs of men and women—to do something we cannot do in our own strength. Today, prayer—calling out to God—is a key to believers practically experiencing the presence and power of the Holy Spirit to change their lives and the situations around them.

Simply put, prayer invites the supernatural into the natural. It is the act of petitioning God to move on our behalf. There are different types of prayer, but for the purpose of this book, suffice it to say that prayer is communion with and supplication to God. Prayer is the power source for supernatural living. If faith is the key, then prayer turns the key and opens the door.

The Scripture says: "The effective, fervent prayer of a righteous man avails much" (James 5:16). This is one of my favorite verses in the Bible. The word *effective* here comes from the Greek word *energeō*, which means to put forth power. It is literally where we get the English word *energy* from. In other words, prayer is the power source for the supernatural. Just as an appliance must be plugged into an outlet in order to generate power, the believer must be plugged into prayer to generate spiritual power that transforms their lives and changes their circumstances.

The Mystery of the Prayer Closet

Jesus taught a profound spiritual principle in the gospel of Matthew. The Bible says, "But you, when you pray, go into your room, and when you have shut your door, pray to your Father who is in the secret place; and your Father who sees in secret will reward you openly" (Matthew 6:6). The word *room*—translated *closet* in the King James Version—comes from the Greek word *tameion*, which means chamber, inner chamber, secret room. This word is actually a Jewish idiom for intimacy between husband and wife (a bed-chamber). Jesus literally tells His disciples to enter into the secret place of intimacy with God to pray. The idea is that of intimacy that leads to conception. We go into the prayer closet and then we engage in intimacy with God until we become impregnated with His power and ultimately give birth to the miraculous.

When Jesus taught about the prayer closet, I don't believe he was simply referring to a physical space, although it can be. Rather, He was talking about a spiritual dimension. What do I mean by this? In the Old Testament, God revealed Himself in the tabernacle in the wilderness. Whenever God wanted to speak to Moses or the Israelites, He would manifest His shekinah glory in the tent. When God would show up in the tabernacle, heaven literally invaded earth and eternity invaded time. This was a type and shadow of prayer today.

The prayer closet is not a physical space, but a spiritual dimension.

The prayer closet is a tent or tabernacle of meeting where we engage God with fervent prayer and worship. It is the place of supplication and intimacy. Requests are made in secret. We speak into the ears of the King in the secret chamber of prayer and make our desires known (even though He knows them anyway). This is why Jesus said, "Therefore I say unto you, What things soever ye desire, when ye pray, believe that ye receive them, and ye shall have them" (Mark 11:24 KJV). Notice that this verse does not make reference to what we need, but to what we "desire." The word *desire* means to ask, beg, call for, crave, require. God is pleased when we ask Him for what we desire. As a father is pleased when His children bring their desires before him, our heavenly Father wants to hear what we want from Him.

But I want to explain this concept of prayer being a spiritual dimension more in depth. The *Oxford Dictionary* defines a dimension as "a measurable extent of some kind, such as length, breadth, depth, or height." As temporal beings we understand reality from four dimensions: length, breadth, depth or height. But God is eternal. He is beyond time and space. When we enter into the place of fervent prayer, we are literally stepping into another dimension, a heavenly dimension that is not confined by time and space. We are communing with an unlimited God who is "able to do exceedingly abundantly above all that we ask or think, according to the power that works in us" (Ephesians 3:20). For instance, in Psalm 91 when it talks about abiding in "the shadow of the Almighty" (verse 1) and taking refuge "under His wings" (verse 4), the psalmist was not speaking of a physical place, but a dimension in God.

Prayer is a dimension where time, space and matter become irrelevant because God is eternal. Have you ever thought about prayer from that perspective? When a loving husband and wife are in their bedchamber during intimacy, it is as if time stands still and nothing else matters. This is the mind frame that we must approach prayer with—He is all that matters.

Ask, Seek, Knock

Jesus said, "Ask, and it shall be given you; seek, and ye shall find; knock, and it shall be opened unto you" (Matthew 7:7 KJV). What if I told you that this was a spiritual model for prayer and to access deeper realms of God's presence and power? In the original Greek this verse actually reads, "Ask and keep on asking, seek and keep on seeking, knock and keep on knocking." Did you notice that the words *ask*, *seek*, and *knock* spell the acronym A.S.K.? I think God was trying to drive the point home. God wants us to persistently approach Him. He wants us to be relentless in prayer until we see the manifestation of what He has promised us.

I am reminded of my oldest son, Isaac. Whenever he wanted something from me, he would ask, and even if the answer was no, he would simply ask in a different way. For example, he would ask, "Daddy, are we going to Chuck E. Cheese?" And I would reply, "I don't think we can go today, Isaac!" So then he would ask, "Can we go tomorrow, Daddy?" And he would keep asking until eventually I would concede to his desires. Does this sound familiar?

In Luke's gospel, Jesus used a parable to teach us how to pray and not lose heart—that is, "always to pray, and not to *faint*" (18:1 KJV, emphasis added):

> "There was in a certain city a judge who did not fear God nor regard man. Now there was a widow in that city; and she came to him, saying, 'Get justice for me from my adversary.' And he would not for a while; but afterward he said within himself, 'Though I do not fear God nor regard man, yet because this widow troubles me I will avenge her, lest by her continual coming she weary me.'"
>
> Then the Lord said, "Hear what the unjust judge said. And shall God not avenge His own elect who cry out day and night to Him, though He bears long with them? I tell you that He will avenge them speedily. Nevertheless, when the Son of Man comes, will He really find faith on the earth?"

> verses 2–8

Jesus taught that we must always pray and not faint. The word *faint* comes from the Greek word *ekkakeō*, which means to be spiritless, wearied or exhausted. Jesus is telling us, don't get exhausted in prayer. Don't lose heart. Keep persisting in prayer until you see the answer. This doesn't mean that we should keep begging God for the same thing, but this does mean that we must stay in faith and thanksgiving until we see what we have asked come to fruition.

We Must Abide in Him

When we talk about miracles, we are not simply talking about sporadic occurrences. We are not talking about random or spontaneous acts of God's power whenever He feels like it. Miracles are a lifestyle that every believer can access once we release our faith and learn to abide in Him.

In the gospel of John, Jesus taught us to abide in Him. In fact, I want to reference this passage of Scripture due to its importance.

> "Abide in Me, and I in you. As the branch cannot bear fruit of itself, unless it abides in the vine, neither can you, unless you abide in Me. . . . If you abide in Me, and My words abide in you, you will ask what you desire, and it shall be done for you."
>
> John 15:4, 7

The word *abide* here means to remain, sojourn or not depart. As we abide in prayer and intimacy, it causes us to be postured in such a way that we are producing fruit. When we abide in prayer, when we ask for what we desire (according to the Word of God) it shall be done. Glory to God!

What do you desire today? What are you believing God to do in your life? Are you willing to abide long enough to see the manifestation? Don't give up! Are you desiring to see miracles? Are you in a place where you believe there is so much more to your Christian life than simply attending church (every now and then)? There is a reality that is available to you, but you have to press into it. You have to be like my son Isaac, who doesn't stop asking, seeking and knocking until he sees his request fulfilled.

Prayer Taps Us into God's Power

Earlier I mentioned that prayer is the divine power source for the believer. This is an important spiritual principle to understand.

Years ago, I remember standing in my kitchen and looking at my blender while daydreaming when the Holy Spirit spoke to me.

Kynan, do you see that blender over there?

I replied, *Yes, Lord!*

He then said to me, *Can it turn on right now?*

I answered, *No, Lord!*

He asked, *Why?*

Because it's not plugged into the socket!

Then God said to me, *Many of My people are not plugged into the power source, and this is why it's not working for them!*

That simple illustration by the Holy Spirit changed my life. I realized that where there is little prayer, there is little power, and where there is much prayer, there is much power. We are commanded to "pray without ceasing" and "hold fast what is good" (1 Thessalonians 5:17, 21). It is through prayer that we tap into the power of God. Prayerlessness is the equivalent to powerlessness.

> **Where there is little prayer, there is little power, and where there is much prayer, there is much power.**

Beloved, every time you pray something happens. Every time we pray, something changes. Just as the engine of a car charges the alternator and allows the battery to be constantly recharged, our prayer life creates the atmosphere that charges our spiritual lives. In fact, Jude says, "But ye, beloved, building up yourselves on your most holy faith, praying in the Holy Ghost, keep yourselves in the love of God" (Jude 1:20–21 KJV). The phrase "building up" in this passage comes from the Greek word *epoikodomeō*, which means to build upon. The root word there literally means to build a house or lay a foundation. In other words, prayer is foundational to our spiritual lives.

Praying in secret allows us to walk in power openly. You can fake many things, but a prayer life or lack thereof is not one of them. When we learn to pray without ceasing, we are tapping into the unlimited eternal power of almighty God! Did you hear what I just said? The New Living Translation of Ephesians 3:20 puts it this way: "Now all glory to God, who is able, through his mighty power at work within us, to accomplish infinitely more than we might ask or think." God is inviting us into a place of prayer and communion with His Holy Spirit that will empower us to operate in the supernatural. He is willing to exceed our greatest expectations and wildest imaginations if we will simply allow His presence and power to work in and through us. Today is the day.

SUMMARY QUESTIONS

1. What is the power source of the supernatural, and why is it necessary?
2. What are you believing God for?
3. How does praying in secret allow us to walk in power publicly?
4. Why does God want us to relentlessly ask in prayer?

MIRACLE ACTIVATION

Father, in the name of Jesus, I thank You for Your presence and power working in and through my life. I recognize that prayer is a power source for the supernatural and through prayer I access dimensions of Your power that I have never experienced before. I declare that I abide in Christ, and His indwelling presence enables me to do the impossible. The miraculous comes easily to me every day because I constantly abide in the "secret place." I believe that through *Your mighty power at work within Me, You will accomplish infinitely more than I can imagine.* In Jesus' name, I pray, Amen.

7

The Power of Proclamation

Open Mouth, Open Heaven

But the centurion replied, "Lord, I am not worthy to have you come under my roof, but only say the word, and my servant will be healed."

Matthew 8:8 ESV

A s He turned aside and gazed at His disciples, a perplexed look filled His visage. This was the first time His disciples ever saw their Master marvel. As they wondered to themselves, He shouted, "Assuredly, I say to you, I have not found such great faith, not even in Israel!" He then turned to the centurion. "Go your way," He declared. "And as you have believed, so let it be done for you."[1]

This classic story found in two of the Synoptic Gospels illustrates the profound power of our Lord, but also the power of Spirit-filled proclamation. When we understand the power of proclamation, it will position us to experience the supernatural in a way that we never have before. What is a proclamation? A proclamation is a public or official announcement, especially one dealing with a matter of great importance. It is also synonymous with declaration. To proclaim is to make a declaration publicly. What does this have to do with walking in the supernatural power of God? I am glad you asked! What we speak carries spiritual power and authority. Contrary to popular belief, what you speak is not inconsequential, but it has a tangible effect on both your spiritual and physical life. This is not some New Age psychobabble. This is biblical truth that has the power to transform your life. You will go from spectating the Scriptures to seeing what the Bible says become a reality.

Our Words Release Supernatural Power

The Bible says, "Death and life are in the power of the tongue, and those who love it will eat its fruit" (Proverbs 18:21). It is very important to understand that your words are powerful and they have the ability to release the supernatural power of God. What kinds of things are you saying? Jesus declared, "It is the Spirit who gives life; the flesh profits nothing. The words that I speak to you are spirit, and they are life" (John 6:63). The words *spirit* and *life* here come from two Greek words, *pneuma* ("spirit"—as in Holy Spirit) and *zōē* ("the absolute fullness of life"). Jesus' words were full of supernatural life and power. Many people think that this was a passage exclusive to Jesus and therefore, it has no relevance to us today, but this would be a very wrong assumption. This is a divine principle. Our words are spiritual. When we speak, our words set spiritual forces in motion. Jesus taught us in Mark 11:22–23 that we would have what we say:

> "Have faith in God. For assuredly, I say to you, whoever says to this mountain, 'Be removed and be cast into the sea,' and does not

doubt in his heart, but believes that those things he says will be done, he will have whatever he says."

This teaching is in response to Peter's observation that the fig tree that He cursed actually withered and died the next day (which is a supernatural phenomenon). Jesus essentially told Peter that if he had faith in God, he would see the same results. What? You mean the works that Jesus did we can do also (see John 14:12)? Absolutely! Have you ever stopped and considered for a moment the power of your words? Many reading this book are still living in the consequences (both positive and negative) of the words that someone spoke over you, whether a teacher, parent, commanding officer, spouse or friend. Something you heard as a child can still resonate with you today. Now consider what would happen if you consistently proclaimed the promises of God over your life and circumstances.

Our Words Shift Spiritual Atmospheres

Then He arose and rebuked the wind, and said to the sea, "Peace, be still!" And the wind ceased and there was a great calm.

Mark 4:39

In the beginning of creation, God established order in the cosmos by declaring His Word. He said, "Let there be light." This was not just a historical account of creation but a spiritual pattern on how atmospheres are transformed by the spoken Word of God. If you want to change the atmosphere of your spiritual life, you must proclaim God's Word. I dare you to say, "I walk in the supernatural power of God every day!" There is something about giving voice to what God has already decreed in His Word. Jesus shifted the atmosphere when He spoke to the wind and the waves declaring, "Peace, be still." The result? "The wind ceased and there was a great calm."

Many people are experiencing fear and anxiety like the disciples were in the midst of the storm. Speak the Word of God over your mind. Declare, "Peace, be still!" The same is true with the chaos that you may be experiencing in your home or on your job. Declare as your heavenly Father did, "Let there be light!"

Proclamation and Manifestation

Today, there are many terms that are often abused or misappropriated. The word *manifestation* is one of them. Later, we will talk about the New Age in more detail, but I want you to know that something coming into manifestation is a spiritual and biblical concept that the enemy has tried to twist and corrupt. When we proclaim the Word of God, it brings the manifestation of God's power, purposes and promises. It is not enough to read your Bible once in a while; you must speak the Word out of your mouth!

I can remember one of my children having a severe umbilical hernia. It was so bad that we thought the child would need surgery, and at the time we didn't have the money or the insurance to afford it. The Lord said to me, *Speak to it!* And that is exactly what I did. I spoke to the hernia and commanded it to shrink and disappear in the name of Jesus. I commanded the muscle tissue to fuse together until the hernia was gone. I literally saw it shrink before my eyes! Glory to God! You may be thinking, *Well, I did that, and nothing happened!* Well, keep speaking! You need to use the P.U.S.H. method. What is the P.U.S.H. method? Proclaim until something happens. Keep proclaiming the Word of God until you see the manifestation. Just as the rock band Journey sang in their hit song "Don't Stop Believin'," we, as believers, should never stop believing! Consistency is a very important key to the supernatural. It's not what you say once in a while, but what you consistently speak that makes the difference.

Our Words Affect Angelic Activity

Did you know that your words are powerful? I know that sounds like a redundant question, seeing I have mentioned it several times, but I want you to really consider the impact our words have on the spiritual realm. Consider Hebrews 1:14: "Are they not all ministering spirits sent forth to minister for those who will inherit salvation?" I firmly believe that our words can effectively engage the spiritual realm and release angelic activity. For instance, the Bible says, "Bless the LORD, you His angels, who excel in strength, who do His word, heeding the voice of His word" (Psalm 103:20). I have heard much debate about the subject of angels. I have heard the teaching that only God can dispatch angels, and not human beings. But according to the book of Psalms, angels (ministering spirits) hearken to "the voice of His word." When we speak God's Word, the angels hearken and act accordingly. We don't need to pray to angels or seek to summon them, but we can say what God says, and when we do, angels are dispatched.

In the book of Genesis, when Abraham prayed for Sodom and Gomorrah (with the intent to save his nephew Lot), God was so moved that He dispatched angels to rescue Lot and his family. It would be easy for us to say that this is an isolated incident in the Bible, but we have countless examples of angels responding to the cries of God's people. In the book of Acts chapter 12, Peter had an angelic visitation in the jail as the church engaged in all night prayer and intercession. Their words provoked a supernatural prison break! I would love to have seen the look on Peter's face as the angel opened the prison doors. Our words are not powerless as many assume, but they are packed with supernatural potential.

What's in a Name?

In the ancient world, it was very common for a person to make a proclamation or sign a legal document in the name of a person of great authority. A name is a term used for identification, or a set of words by which a person is known. Jesus said, "If you ask anything in My name, I will do it" (John 14:14). The word *name* here comes from the Greek word *onoma*, which means "the name is used for everything which the name covers, everything the thought or feeling of which is aroused in the mind by mentioning, hearing and remembering the name (i.e., for one's rank, authority, interests, pleasure, command, excellences, deeds, etc.)." When we talk about asking something in someone's name, we are talking about asking in their character or their authority. In the ancient world, if you came in the name of someone, that meant you carried their authority. You had a relationship with that person. You could not come in the name of Caesar if Caesar didn't know you. When you say "in the name of" something, what you are saying is, "I come in the authority of that name." Wow! Likewise, if you had the signet ring of an official, it's as if the official had signed the document themselves. In other words, if you were to take someone's signet ring, that means you have power of attorney.

What Jesus' Name Really Means

As we have shared in this chapter, our words have the profound ability to affect the world around us. This truth is even more amplified by the reality that we as believers have been given an omnipotent weapon and key to unlocking the supernatural power of God in greater dimensions. We have the name of Jesus! Why is the name of Jesus so powerful and important, and what does His name mean? More importantly, what does the name of Jesus have to do with miracles? Everything! The Bible says,

> Therefore God also has highly exalted Him and given Him the name which is above every name, that at the name of Jesus every knee should bow, of those in heaven, and of those on earth, and of

those under the earth, and that every tongue should confess that Jesus Christ is Lord, to the glory of God the Father.

Philippians 2:9–11

Jesus conquered death, hell and the grave and has been exalted to the highest name in the cosmos—there is no other name more powerful than His. "In Jesus' name" is not just a phrase we use in church; it's a spiritual understanding—that's why some people say it and nothing happens (see Acts 19:13–16). They don't have a revelation of or a relationship with the name they are invoking. When we make proclamations in Jesus' name, we are actually stepping into His power and authority. We walk in that authority from a place of relationship and identity. We know Him and are known by Him, therefore we have the right to use His name. Demons flee at the mention of His name. Sickness bows at the mention of His name. Miracles break forth at the mention of His name. We are not just using "Christianese" when we say the name Jesus. Something literally shifts in the atmosphere when we declare His name. Simply put, there is power in the name of Jesus. If you are going to live in the miraculous consistently, you must declare His name.

Spiritual Power of Attorney

I want to expound further on the profound power of the name of Jesus. When we pray or declare in the name of Jesus, we are acting as power of attorney for the Kingdom of heaven. What is power of attorney? Power of attorney is the authority to act for another person in specified or all legal or financial matters. When a person has power of attorney, they are the legal agent of the person whose name they represent. Legally speaking, they can act on behalf of another with such veracity that it is as if the person is acting themselves. Think about what I just said! To pray or declare in the name of Jesus is to stand in His place as His legal representative. In actuality, Jesus is our Advocate in heaven, and we are His ambassadors on the earth. So when Jesus prayed for miracles, He did so with confidence knowing that His unbroken union with the Father guaranteed Him answers to prayer. When we pray, we are praying from the posture of the relationship that Jesus has with the Father, not just the relationship that we perceive that we have with Jesus. This is the reason miracles happen in His name, because when we speak in His name, the Miracle Worker Himself shows up. Glory to God! In the ancient world, a king would delegate his signet ring to sign official documents or make official proclamations. The name of Jesus is the signet ring of heaven. When we pray or declare in the name of Jesus, we are utilizing the signet ring of the King—praying in the name of Jesus, with the authority of the King in His Kingdom.

Open Mouth, Open Heaven

I remember growing up around people from the southern part of the United States, and they always had these colloquial expressions. One of them I vividly remember was, "A closed mouth won't get fed!" This simply meant that if you wanted something, you should say something. In fact, I had a neighbor whose mother would always cook delicious food. After school, I would go by his house, and it smelled like a restaurant inside. She would always say, "Kynan, I made some brownies, do you want some?" Our culture discouraged asking other people for food, but I couldn't help but give in to the power of the aroma that exuded from the oven. Finally, with a quivering lip, I would say, "Yes, ma'am!" Then she would say, "A closed mouth won't get fed! Speak up next time!" Little did I know that I was being equipped spiritually. In the Kingdom of God, an open mouth equals an open heaven.

Jesus taught His disciples in Matthew 16:19, "And I will give you the keys of the kingdom of heaven, and whatever you bind on earth will be bound in heaven, and whatever you loose on earth will be loosed in heaven." Notice that this statement is in response to what Peter said: "Simon Peter answered and *said*, 'You are the Christ, the Son of the living God'" (Matthew 16:16, emphasis added). The Greek word for *said* here is *eipon*, which means to speak or to say. Peter opened his mouth and declared the revelation of Jesus Christ. This was a spiritual key. The word *key* comes from the Greek word *kleis*, which means power and authority of various kinds or the ability to open various doors. Literally, when we open our mouth in the name (authority) of Jesus, the heavens respond accordingly. Indeed, an open mouth is an open heaven!

I challenge you today: Open your mouth and declare God's Word. Declare the breakthrough! Declare the healing! The enemy wants you to believe the lie that your words don't mean anything, but it's not true. Heaven is waiting on you to speak.

The Miracle in Your Mouth

"For assuredly, I say to you, whoever says to this mountain, 'Be removed and be cast into the sea,' and does not doubt in his heart, but believes that those things he says will be done, he will have whatever he says."

Mark 11:23

We are living in an age when people have faced so much discouragement (we will talk about how to overcome discouragement in a later chapter), but I want to remind you that God's Word is true and it is the final authority. We must cleave to the Word of God despite the sway of the culture. The Bible says that we will have what we say. Do you believe that? If I told you that you would have everything you say, would you still say the same things you are saying today? Friends, your miracle is in your mouth!

I remember a particular boy in our congregation had a severe case of vitiligo on his head. This is a skin condition that causes depigmentation of the skin. There is no known cure for this condition, although steroids are often prescribed to reduce the appearance and prevent it from spreading further. His mother came to me one day, and I asked her how long he'd had the condition. She told me he'd had it for a while. I simply said, "Jesus can fix that!" Weeks later, the vitiligo disappeared! Glory to God!

We have seen countless miracles such as this one over the years. It is much simpler than people realize. You can experience the supernatural in every area of your life if you embrace the truth that the miraculous is your portion. A miracle does not take place in a vacuum. Heaven moves when earth places a demand. When we speak faith-filled words into the atmosphere, something happens. I believe the miracle that many are looking for is one proclamation away.

SUMMARY QUESTIONS

1. What is a Spirit-filled proclamation?
2. How can words shift an atmosphere?
3. Why are the words "in Jesus' name" more than just a phrase?
4. If I told you that you would have everything you say, what would you say today?

MIRACLE ACTIVATION

Father, in the name of Jesus, I recognize that life and death are in the power of the tongue and that my words have the ability to shift and transform the atmosphere. Your Word declares that we shall decree a thing and it would be established; therefore I decree that the heavens are opened above every area of my life. I declare that the Word of God dispatches angels; therefore as I proclaim the Word of God, I receive divine assistance in every area of my life. I declare that my family, finances, friendships, and endeavors are blessed and supernaturally accelerated by the power of God's Word. I declare that the goodness of God follows me all the days of my life, in the name of Jesus. Amen.

8

Breaking Free from Guilt and Shame

Overcoming the Theology of Unworthiness

She said, "No one, Lord." And Jesus said to her, "Neither do I condemn you; go and sin no more."

John 8:11

The mob shouted louder and louder as the crowds grew. The commotion was so great that it resembled a storm. As the men of the city marched out of the house, dragging the woman by her tattered clothes into the middle of town, her cries could be heard from hundreds of feet away. She had been caught in the act of adultery.

The religious leaders surrounded her, stones in their hands. Then they brought her to the man called Jesus. "The law says that this woman ought to be stoned!" they shouted. "What do *You* say?"

There was complete silence. Then suddenly His words pierced the atmosphere. "Let him who is without sin cast the first stone." One by one, stones began to drop, and you could hear a syncopation so consistent it resembled an orchestra. His next words to the disgraced woman were both perplexing and refreshing. "Where are your accusers? Neither do I condemn you. Go and sin no more!"

The story of the woman caught in adultery is a powerful example of the mercy of God (see John 7:53–8:11). In this account, Jesus did not condone her sin, but He withheld the judgment that she deserved. He refused to condemn her for her sin. Jesus displayed the heart of the Father.

What does this have to do with miracles? Everything! Many Christians struggle with the miraculous because they struggle with guilt and shame. As a result of this shame and guilt, they find themselves unable to confidently walk in the power of God. They wonder, *How could God ever use me?* Have you ever thought this way? This creates a mindset of fear and insecurity. What if I told you that God doesn't want to use you at all? What if I told you that God desires to partner with you to see His power displayed through you? As a person who spent a large portion of my Christian life struggling with feelings of guilt, I know firsthand the destructive cycle that shame creates.

Overcoming the Theology of Unworthiness

Years ago, I had a profound spiritual experience. As I stood under a palm tree, the leaves of the tree began to blow vigorously, and I heard a voice speak: *Sin shall not have dominion over you, for you are not under the law but under grace!* (Romans 6:14). I call this my "Florida burning palm tree experience," although the tree was not burning. For the first time in my Christian life, I understood what grace really meant. I understood that sin would no longer dominate my spiritual life—because I was no longer under the law. It was not a matter of overcoming sin so that I would then be eligible for grace—it was about receiving grace so that I could live in the victory over sin that was won for me. This was a pivotal moment in my spiritual life, and it was the framework from which God was able to build my confidence to walk in the supernatural. Like the woman who was caught in adultery, I was now empowered to overcome the power of sin, guilt, shame and condemnation and walk in my true identity as a child of God.

Unfortunately, many believers have a theology of unworthiness; that is, a belief system that suggests that they are wretched sinners, unworthy of God's love and acceptance. Not only is this unbiblical, but it is extremely disempowering. If you don't know that God loves you, how will you confidently partner with God to release His supernatural power? Hebrews 10:14 tells us, "For by one offering He has perfected forever those who are being sanctified." My friend, if you are a sincere believer in Jesus, that includes you. It is false humility to say you are a wretched sinner when the blood of Jesus was shed to sanctify you. In fact, if you don't accept the work of the cross of Christ as the only efficacious sacrifice capable of redeeming mankind, despite your frailty and sin, you are suggesting that the cross was not enough. God forbid!

These are a few things the Bible says about you:

- You are justified and glorified (see Romans 8:30).
- You have been chosen in Him before the foundation of the world (see Ephesians 1:4).
- You have been blessed with heavenly blessings (see Ephesians 1:3).
- He has made you to sit together with Him in heavenly places (see Ephesians 2:6).
- You are a joint heir with Christ (see Romans 8:17).

The Bible says, "And if children, then heirs—heirs of God and joint heirs with Christ, if indeed we suffer with Him, that we may also be glorified together" (Romans 8:17). One of the most profound truths of the New Testament is the biblically irrefutable fact that we are joint heirs of Jesus Christ. The word *joint heir* comes from the Greek word *sygklēronomos*, which means in a literal sense one who obtains "something assigned to himself with others, a joint participant." This word only appears once in the New Testament, but the concept of being an heir with Christ or co-participant with Christ is all throughout the New Testament. We have been buried with Christ, co-crucified with Christ, co-resurrected with Christ and co-seated with Him in heavenly places: "But God . . . made us alive together with Christ (by grace you have been saved), and raised us up together, and made us sit together in the heavenly places in Christ Jesus" (Ephesians 2:4–6).

We have received an inheritance in Christ and with Christ. This is the antithesis of unworthiness. We were made worthy by His blood and justified freely by His grace. On the basis of this alone, we have received access to heavenly realms. The cross and resurrection is the evidence of our authoritative right to walk in the power of God. Once we place our faith and trust in Christ, we have access to all the fullness of God. Glory to God! Did you hear what I just said? You are not a victim. You are not a slave. You are not a second-class citizen in the Kingdom of God.

Why are these things so important to understand? Without a foundational understanding of Christology (the doctrine of Christ), it is impossible to understand who He is and who we are, and what we have received as a result of His sacrifice. Without this renewed mindset, it will also be impossible to walk in an authentic demonstration of the supernatural as our inheritance. As we have stated before, miracles do not flow from our own effort or self-righteousness, but from the Person of Jesus. Miracles are part of our spiritual inheritance.

Self-Condemnation: Spiritual Sabotage

Earlier, we talked about our inheritance in Christ, and how this inheritance grants us confidence to walk as sons and daughters of God, in the sense that we are able to invite people around us into genuine manifestations of the presence and power of God. If we know that God loves us, we should want everyone around us to know that He loves them as well. One of the hindrances to this is self-condemnation, which is a form of spiritual sabotage. The enemy uses self-condemnation as a weapon.

What is self-condemnation? Essentially, condemnation is a damnatory sentence. It comes from the Greek root word *katakrinō*, which means to judge someone worthy of punishment. Self-condemnation, therefore, is the belief that you are not worthy of forgiveness or mercy, but instead that you are worthy of judgment or punishment. This is not to be mistaken with contrition or godly sorrow. We should always experience a deep remorse when we have sinned against God. As His children, we have the desire to please Him in every area of our lives. When we are operating in "self-condemnation," however, we are telling God that the blood of Jesus is insufficient as a ransom for our sin. This is why many Christians are not walking in the supernatural: They don't believe that God can use them. To this point, I want to share an interesting testimony.

Years ago, I was ministering in Australia. I was about to speak at a small church in New South Wales. As I walked toward the pulpit, I prayed a very simple prayer that I often pray: "God, use me for Your glory!" The response I heard shocked me. *I don't want to use you!* the Lord said. When He spoke those words to me, I was devastated. I thought surely that I was in trouble. I asked God why. Had I become a reprobate? The Lord said to me, *Son, I don't want to simply use you. I want to partner with you!* He went further to say, *Anything that is used can be discarded.* I knew at that very moment that God was challenging my mindset. He wanted to teach me that our relationship is a partnership.

So when the devil comes to you and tells you that God will not use you, tell the devil, "You are right! He would much rather partner with me!" Faith is confidence in God's Word, but when we are in self-condemnation, we lack the confidence to do what we're called to do and be who we're called to be.

Guilt, Shame and Comparison

Next, I'd like to talk about the destructive power of guilt, shame and comparison. It is my personal conviction that there is almost nothing more destructive to the life of a believer than guilt, shame and comparison. I am sure that you are probably thinking that the most destructive thing to a believer is sin, and you would be partially correct. Although the wages of sin is death according to Romans 6:23, the reality is that Jesus paid the ultimate price to destroy the power of sin. His blood was the propitiation for our sin (see Romans 3:25). The word *propitiation* here comes from the Greek word *hilastērion*, which means "relating to an appeasing or expiating, having placating or expiating force, expiatory; a means of appeasing or expiating, a propitiation." Expiation is the act of making amends or reparation for guilt or wrongdoing; atonement. Jesus' sacrifice removed the guilt and shame associated with sin. The blood of Jesus has turned condemnation and wrath away from us. This is why guilt is so destructive to the believer, because it seeks to nullify the work of the cross.

When we live in guilt, we live under the power of the very sin Jesus came to deliver us from. Moreover, guilt causes people to reject the implications of the sacrifice of Jesus, because they do not believe that they qualify. Thus the accuser of the brethren is constantly seeking to use guilt as a weapon to destroy the confidence of God's children. Again, by guilt I am not talking about the regret that we should feel when we sin, but the "damnatory sentence" that one lives under as a result of sin. If the devil can get you to believe that the reason you are sick is because God is punishing you or teaching you a lesson, then he can effectively convince you to abdicate your spiritual authority as a believer. Furthermore, if you live under the power of guilt, you won't release the miraculous. Why? Because you will not believe that you qualify. The accusing whispers of the enemy will come to you telling you that you are the wrong person to pray for someone else. *You aren't spiritual enough!* he tells you. But these are lies! Guilt leads to shame.

"Then you shall know that I am in the midst of Israel: I am the LORD your God and there is no other. My people shall never be put to shame."

Joel 2:27

Typically, when the Bible speaks of shame, it is in a negative context. When we are living in the guilt of sin, this produces the shame that brings disappointment and confusion. In the Garden of Eden, Adam and Eve were naked and unashamed—meaning they were not disconcerted or confounded even though they weren't wearing clothing. Imagine someone walking into a public restroom where you were undressed. I am sure that would be an embarrassing experience for most of us. Adam and Eve were never ashamed before God's presence. Why? They were more aware of God's presence than themselves. But when sin came into the picture, this sin brought shame. They attempted to hide from God's presence. In the very next generation (Cain and Abel), we see the progressive consequences of sin in the form of comparison. Cain compared himself to Abel (his younger brother) and allowed his heart to be filled with jealousy, which ultimately led to murder. When we walk in guilt, guilt brings shame, and shame brings comparison.

Beloved, you don't have to live in this destructive cycle. You don't have to compare yourself to others in a way that makes you insecure about God's ability to work with and through you. The mold was broken with you. The gifts He has imparted to you are unique and important. But you must stand in the righteousness of Jesus Christ.

I don't know about you, but words cannot express my gratitude for the fact that God is merciful. I know that the message of holiness and righteousness are so necessary in the times in which we live, but we should never forget to emphasize the grace and mercy of God. Simply put, your past does not disqualify you from the miraculous. If you have failed in your past, you are still eligible to become a partner with God in His agenda to release heaven on earth. The blood of Jesus is so powerful that it has cleansed us from our sin. Do you believe this truth? The Bible does! "But if we walk in the light as He is in the light, we have fellowship with one another, and the blood of Jesus Christ His Son cleanses us from all sin" (1 John 1:7).

Your past does not disqualify you from the miraculous.

Oftentimes, it is difficult for us to overcome the past because we are constantly reminded of our past by people and circumstances around us. The devil constantly reminds us of the past to get us to feel disqualified. But the Bible says this: "Therefore if any man be in Christ, he is a new creature: old things are passed away; behold, all things are become new" (2 Corinthians 5:17). Did you know that you are a new creation in Christ? What does that mean? It means that you are a different species of being than you were before (spiritually speaking). You are born again. The past is no more.

God wants to manifest Himself in and through you despite your past. This is great news! If God can use Paul, who was a murderer, to write 80 percent of the New Testament, then you can only imagine what He can do with you. In fact, the greatest miracle in the cosmos is the miracle of salvation. Our faith in Christ has made us new. Glory to God!

Blessed is he whose transgression is forgiven, whose sin is covered. Blessed is the man to whom the LORD does not impute iniquity, and in whose spirit there is no deceit. When I kept silent, my bones grew old through my groaning all the day long. For day and night Your hand was heavy upon me; my vitality was turned into the drought of summer. Selah. I acknowledged my sin to You, and my iniquity I have not hidden. I said, "I will confess my transgressions to the LORD," and You forgave the iniquity of my sin.

Psalm 32:1–5

Here are a few other Scriptures on condemnation:

- Psalm 103:12: "As far as the east is from the west, so far has He removed our transgressions from us."
- Psalm 34:22: "The LORD redeems the souls of His servants, and none of those who take refuge in Him will be condemned" (NASB1995).
- 2 Corinthians 7:10: "For godly sorrow produces repentance leading to salvation, not to be regretted; but the sorrow of the world produces death."
- Matthew 18:21–22: "'Lord, how often shall my brother sin against me, and I forgive him? Up to seven times?' Jesus said to him, 'I do not say to you, up to seven times, but up to seventy times seven.'"[1]

As believers, we must learn how to break the cycle of guilt, shame and condemnation, so I want to take another moment and define those terms for the purposes of this book.

When we talk about guilt, we are speaking about "the fact of having committed a specified or implied offense or crime." Shame is "a painful feeling of humiliation or distress caused by the consciousness of wrong or foolish behavior." Condemnation is a pronouncement of guilt or punishment, to declare to be reprehensible, wrong or evil usually after weighing evidence and without reservation. Guilt, shame and condemnation are rooted in unforgiveness toward yourself.

Have you ever thought about it this way? Did you know that when you refuse to forgive yourself, you are walking in pride? When people refuse to forgive, they are essentially saying that the blood of Jesus was not enough. Instead, we are called to forgive ourselves: "For if you forgive men their trespasses, your heavenly Father will also forgive you. But if you do not forgive men their trespasses, neither will your Father forgive your trespasses" (Matthew 6:14–15). He paid too high a price for us to be in shame, guilt or condemnation.

Guilt says, *I am not forgiven!* Condemnation says, *I am worthy of judgment!* Shame says, *That is still who I am!* We have to come to the realization that nothing we did today or yesterday will keep us from the forgiveness of sins once we repent with a sincere heart.

Keys to Moving Forward

There is good news that you need to hear: God is a gracious and merciful God who loves you unconditionally. The truth is that you have a rich inheritance in Christ and you have been called to be an ambassador of heaven. God desires to partner with you to express His power and presence. There are a few keys that I want to share with you that will help you be confident that you are in right standing with God.

The Bible says, "He who covers his sins will not prosper, but whoever confesses and forsakes them will have mercy" (Proverbs 28:13). The enemy of your soul is the accuser of the brethren. He loves to bring up past sins to keep you tethered to your old life. Whenever you feel guilt rising up, ask the Holy Spirit if there is any area of your life that requires confession of sin and repentance. And remember that the Bible says to "confess your trespasses to one another, and pray for one another, that you may be healed. The effective, fervent prayer of a righteous man avails much" (James 5:16).

There is an old adage, "Tell the truth and shame the devil!" This statement is true in the sense that Satan is the father of lies. We combat the lies of the enemy with the truth of God's Word and by being honest when we fall short. According to the Word of God, we receive healing when we confess our faults and pray for one another. Once you have done this, declare, "My sin is in the depths of the sea!"—and don't go diving for it anymore. Finally, you must meditate on the Word of God as a constant reminder of your new identity in Christ. You are qualified because the work of the cross was efficacious. Glory to God!

SUMMARY QUESTIONS

1. What are the hindrances to walking in the supernatural power of God's love?
2. Why is it important to break the cycle of guilt, shame and condemnation?
3. What are keys to moving forward from the shame of sin?
4. What does the Bible say we must do in order to receive healing from sin?

MIRACLE ACTIVATION

Father, I thank You for Your steadfast love toward me. Your Word declares that Your mercy endures forever. In You I have been born again—a new creation. The past is no more. I declare that my life is free from the shackles of guilt, shame and condemnation. I declare that I live in the fullness of Your grace, and Your grace enables me to walk in the supernatural and live a life of freedom and victory. I declare that sin has no dominion over my life, for I am not under the law, but under grace. I live in the inexhaustible grace of God. I operate in miracles daily! In Jesus' name, Amen.

9

Hope

The Anchor of the Soul

This hope we have as an anchor of the soul, both sure and steadfast, and which enters the Presence behind the veil.

Hebrews 6:19

The multitudes were so close you could hardly move, the noise of chatter so loud you could no longer distinguish the voices. Many years had passed by without any hope of healing, but today something was different. A palpable presence filled the atmosphere. Today she had a new expectancy in her heart.

The woman told herself, *If I can just touch the borders of His garment, I will be made whole!* So she took a risk she had never taken before. The law demanded isolation, but her hope compelled her to action. She stepped out and pressed through the crowd, her confidence growing with each step.

Finally, she fixed her gaze on Him. It all seemed like a dream. Every fiber in her being leapt forward to touch Him, and suddenly, everything changed. A joy filled her heart that she had never experienced in her life.

Jesus turned and said, "Who touched Me?"

And there she knelt, heart racing, as she gazed into the face of the Messiah. In an instant, her hopelessness had turned to healing.

I love the story of the woman with the issue of blood found in the Synoptic Gospels. Her story is one of hope and victory. She was able to believe in the promise of God against all odds. This story illustrates the necessity and power of hope in walking in the miraculous.

The Bible says, "Now faith is the substance of things hoped for, the evidence of things not seen" (Hebrews 11:1). We will speak more about faith in a later chapter, but I want to draw attention to the word *hope* here. It comes from the Greek word *elpizō* and implies waiting on something with joyful and confident expectation. Scripture says that faith is actually the substance of our hope. I like to define it this way: Faith is your confidence in God's Word, but hope is your anticipation of a future promise.

> **Faith is your confidence in God's Word, but hope is your anticipation of a future promise.**

The Bible tells us that the woman with the issue of blood "said within herself," *If I touch the borders of His garment, I will be made whole* (Matthew 9:21 KJV). After years of disappointment, she held on to hope, and that hope tethered her to God's promise despite her circumstances. The writer of Hebrews calls hope the "anchor of the soul" (6:19). I believe that many people in the Church deal with disappointment because the things they have looked forward to have not come to pass. I believe hope is a vital key to tapping into the supernatural power of God and releasing miracles. Get ready to hope again!

The Attitude of Expectancy

Essentially, hope is a confident expectation that God is going to do something good in the future. I often like to say, "Something good is going to happen!" Like the woman with the issue of blood in Matthew, we must have a confident expectation that God will do something supernatural in us, for us and through us. Hallelujah! I call this an attitude of expectancy. We must live in a state of constant anticipation that something supernatural can and will break forth at any moment to the glory of God. Whether we are in the classroom or the church, we must believe that God desires to invade the space we are in at any moment and manifest His favor, power and love.

It reminds me of my children; when they were much younger, I would watch them stir up their own excitement. One of my children would tell the others, "I think Daddy might take us to the zoo today!" Moments later, they were describing how the animals look in the cages while screaming in excitement and anticipation. It was as if they could see the entire experience in their mind. This is called expectancy.

The attitude of expectancy creates the atmosphere for miracles. Make no mistake, your attitude is absolutely critical. Are you optimistic about the future? Do you believe that the miracles in the Bible will take place in your life? Do you wake up in the morning looking forward to the testimonies that will come about? Or do you have a cynical attitude?

God's Word is full of promises. When expectancy mingles with the Word, it produces miracles. Here are some scriptural references for your encouragement:

> For we are saved by hope: but hope that is seen is not hope: for what a man seeth, why doth he yet hope for? But if we hope for that we see not, then do we with patience wait for it.
>
> Romans 8:24–25 KJV

Now the God of hope fill you with all joy and peace in believing, that ye may abound in hope, through the power of the Holy Ghost.

Romans 15:13 KJV

If the Bible says that He is the God of hope, then it stands to reason that we ought to be people filled with hope. What does it mean to have hope as an anchor of the soul? An anchor is defined as "a heavy object attached to a rope or chain and used to moor a vessel to the sea bottom, typically one having a metal shank with a ring at one end for the rope and a pair of curved and/or barbed flukes at the other." The purpose of an anchor is to tether the vessel to the ocean floor to keep the boat from drifting away. The anchor has to have enough weight to keep the vessel stable, or it will be carried away by the waves. Our hope must have enough weight to keep us connected to the firm foundation of God's Word. We must stay anchored to the Word of God at all times. As you read this chapter, I believe your hope will be stirred and that you will receive an impartation of a spirit of expectancy. Please remember this: Something good is going to happen to you.

Something good is going to happen to you.

Overcoming Hope Deferred

Many Christians don't have a lack of faith but a lack of hope because of disappointment, the loss of a loved one, sickness, hardship or other difficult circumstances. As a result of this hopelessness, the enemy has convinced them that nothing can or will ever change. This is a lie from the pit of hell. The Bible says, "Hope deferred maketh the heart sick: but when the desire cometh, it is a tree of life" (Proverbs 13:12 KJV). In other words, when a person has expected to receive something that has not come to fruition in a long time, it causes them to contract the disease called hope-lessness. The word *deferred* comes from the Hebrew word *māšak*, which means to drag along, prolong or continue.

Friends, you must understand that delay is not synonymous with denial. Keep expecting! We must be like my children in my earlier illustration. You must have a mental picture of what you believe God can and will do. When the enemy comes to distort that picture and cause you to drift away, hold on to the anchor. Maybe you have a loved one you have been praying for and after several years, they are still not healed of that sickness. Maybe you have been believing for a wayward child to come to the Lord. Regardless, don't lose hope. I believe that your "dead hope" is being resurrected again. Hold on to the truth that God is able and willing. Maybe you have desired to step out in faith and walk in the supernatural, but every time you attempt to minister to some-one, nothing happens. Keep stepping out. Something is going to happen!

Hopeful Expectancy Releases Miracles

As I mentioned earlier, whatever we posture ourselves to expect, we look forward to receiving. Imagine a wide receiver on the football field. If he is to catch the throw from the quarterback, he must be open and anticipating the catch. Heaven desires to throw a touch-down every single day, but are you "open" and "anticipating"? The posture of hopeful expectancy is the key to releasing miracles. You don't get what you deserve. You get what you expect.

I vividly remember an interesting experience I had related to expectancy. I was preaching in a small church in California, and during the night service, a woman with cerebral palsy was brought in. She had not walked normally since she was born. She was ushered to the front with her walker so she could receive prayer. I could hear the devil mocking, *She is not going to get healed! Just look at her!* But something kept pulling me to contend for her healing. She was full of expectancy. It was as if her expectation was drawing on the anointing operating through me. The Lord prompted me to walk up to her and whisper in her ear, "You can do all things through Christ who strengthens you!" The more I spoke the truth of God's Word into her ear, the more she began to walk, and the more the crowd shouted in excitement. Then I slowly removed the walker from her hand. Again, I said to her, "You can do all things through Christ who strengthens you!" With every declaration, I would take a step with her while holding her hand. I said this several times in her ear until, finally, she began to run around the church without any walker or device. Glory to God!

From this powerful testimony, you can see that one of the keys to the woman receiving her healing from cerebral palsy was not just expectancy alone. Rather, it was the words spoken into her ear that fueled her excitement about the miracle that God desired to give her.

Excited and Ignited

If expectation charges the atmosphere, then excitement is the ignition that causes an explosion of miracles. Simply put, when we get excited, we get ignited. When we get ignited, miracles go *boom*. Glory! There is something that I like to call divine provocation. The more you talk about miracles, the more excited and ignited you get about seeing those miracles in your life and the lives of the people around you.

Think about it like a person talking about a nice restaurant. The more you talk about what you're about to eat, the more your mouth waters in anticipation. You can taste the food before you arrive at the restaurant. The same is true of our spiritual lives. Conversation creates expectation. Think about it this way: A conversation cost the human race intimate fellowship and connection with God and the Garden of Eden itself. If sinful conversations can cause such devastating spiritual (and sometimes physical) consequences, what positive effects would one experience by engaging in edifying and biblical conversations about the power and presence of God?

The Bible tells us, "And let us consider one another to provoke unto love and to good works" (Hebrews 10:24 KJV). We are called by God to provoke one another as it relates to spiritual things. This is why our testimony is so powerful. When we tell people of the goodness of God, and how He works in our lives, people begin to inquire and desire more of God in the various areas of their lives.

> **The more you talk about miracles, the more excited and ignited you get about seeing those miracles in your life and the lives of the people around you.**

I can even remember a testimony I heard about God using someone to heal a brother of cancer. It provoked me so much that I began to tell God, "If You could operate through them in that way, You can operate through me the same way!" One day, I was invited to pray for a man who was recently diagnosed with a severe and very advanced cancer. He was given three months to live. When I saw him, the cancer had already metastasized all over his body. I asked him if he wanted to live. He insisted that he did. As I laid my hand on his head, I felt the prompting of the Holy Spirit to rebuke the spirit of death. In short, that was over a decade ago, and as of the time of the writing of this book, he is still alive. God is so faithful! Are you getting ignited yet?

The Dangers of Discouragement

Have you ever seen a shriveled-up raisin or other dried piece of fruit? It's tough and hard, right? Many Christians are like that raisin: They have become spiritually dry due to discouragement. What is discouragement? The dictionary defines *discouragement* as a "loss of confidence or enthusiasm; dispiritedness." Does this sound familiar? The actual root word for discouragement comes from the French word *descouragier*, which is derived from two Latin words, *des* (away) and *corage* (courage). Discouragement, therefore, comes when a believer allows the enemy to either distance themselves from courage or take their courage away. Discouragement leads to despair.

Have you ever talked to believers who often reference "the good old days" when God did wonderful things through them? Sadly, today they don't have the zeal or the passion for God that they once had. This is what we call discouragement. If unchecked, it will become cynicism and ultimately despondency. God wants to do even greater than what He did in the past. Amen? You must make a conscious decision that you will not live in a prison of discouragement. The Bible gives us an example of what we should do when we face the temptation to be discouraged: "Now David was greatly distressed, for the people spoke of stoning him, because the soul of all the people was grieved, every man for his sons and his daughters. But David strengthened himself in the LORD his God" (1 Samuel 30:6). Make the decision that God is more than able and more than willing to keep His word.

Coming Alive Again

I believe the Church is on the precipice of the greatest awakening in the history of the human race. If that sounds to you like a grand statement, you are absolutely right, but it is true. Just as Ezekiel prophesied to the dry bones (see Ezekiel 37), we are on the brink of a spiritual resurrection of hope in the body of Christ. The question that God asked Ezekiel is being posed to the Church today: "Can these dry bones live again?" The Holy Spirit is speaking life and hope into the Church (meaning you) once again. Maybe you are someone who has in some ways allowed their hope to become dry. If so, I prophesy to those dry bones and command them to come alive again, just as God spoke to the nation of Israel in the Old Testament. Be careful not to get dry or stay dry. Come alive in the name of Jesus!

One of the ways that we ignite our expectancy is by asking ourselves what God is doing in our lives today. Miracles from the past are great, but we need to see miracles today! We cannot settle for spiritual nostalgia. God is challenging the Church today to believe Him for more. Miracles are for today and they are for now. Jesus Christ is the same yesterday and today and forever (see Hebrews 13:8). If He could do it then, He can do it again. He is still working miracles for those who will believe.

There are some practical things that we can do to keep ourselves "fresh" in the Holy Spirit. How do we avoid becoming dry? We can ignite our spiritual lives and avoid spiritual drought by worship, by reading the Word of God and by engaging in challenging conversations with other believers. I say again, don't let your expectancy dry up. When was the last time you prayed for someone to be healed? And I don't mean a silent prayer, but when you had to inconvenience yourself to do it. Ask God to give you insight into ways He desires to work in and through you for His glory.

Remove the Lid

When I was a young man, I enjoyed going to a particular shopping mall in Atlanta. There was a little Christian-owned restaurant inside the mall that people really loved. This restaurant specialized in fried chicken sandwiches and fresh hand-squeezed lemonade. Today, they are a multibillion-dollar company known all over the world, but back then they were not as well known. Anyway, they had a policy of free refills. I loved lemonade, so this was a tremendous blessing for me. There was one condition, however: You had to remove the lid off the cup yourself in order for them to give you a refill.

As I think about this conversation about releasing miracles, the phrase "Remove the lid!" comes to mind. I believe that God desires to pour out His Spirit and power on the Church like never before, but we must first "remove the lid" (the limitations) and allow God to manifest His glory to the full extent He desires. He is not intimidated by your desire for more, but He longs to fill your cup to overflowing.

Have you been discouraged by the apparent lack of manifestation in your spiritual life? Just ask. Jesus admonished us to "ask, and it will be given to you; seek, and you will find; knock, and it will be opened to you" (Matthew 7:7). There is something supernatural about asking God for more and not being content with where you are in your spiritual life right now. Now is the time and today is the day for you to experience the supernatural power of God.

SUMMARY QUESTIONS

1. What is hope, and how does it bring an atmosphere of miracles?
2. Why is it so dangerous to become "spiritually dry"?
3. How does a believer avoid spiritual drought?
4. Where in your life do you need to be resurrected?

MIRACLE ACTIVATION

Father, in the name of Jesus, I thank You for Your presence in my life. I know that hope is a confident expectation of something good. Your Word says that hope is the anchor of the soul. I, therefore, declare that I have a lively hope in Your Word. I declare that I possess an attitude of expectancy and this attitude creates an atmosphere of the miraculous in my life. Just as God spoke to the Israelites, I prophesy to dry bones and command them to come alive again. I declare I will not get dry or stay dry. Make me come alive, fill me with an attitude of hopeful expectancy and give me insight into ways You desire to work in and through me for Your glory. In Jesus' name, Amen.

10

Action Activates Miracles

Take the Leap

Peter answered Him and said, "Lord, if it is You, command me to come to You on the water." So He said, "Come." And when Peter had come down out of the boat, he walked on the water to go to Jesus.

Matthew 14:28–29

It was one of the most frightening nights they had ever experienced. The wind was so strong that their ship nearly capsized. They had never experienced such a tempest. Suddenly, out of the darkness of the storm they could see the figure of a man walking on the sea. Were they dreaming? Was this a ghost? As the man drew closer, the disciples became more afraid. Peter looked closer and recognized Him as the Master. In an unusual feat, he stood on the edge of the boat and exclaimed, "Master, if it is You, please bid me to come!" The Master responded, "It is I! Come!"

With raw faith, he responded to the Master's words and stepped out of the boat. In defiance of every natural law known to man, he walked on water.

In chapter 2, we referenced the story of Peter walking on water as recorded in the book of Matthew chapter 14. We coined the term *Water Walkers*. I bring up this example again because I believe it perfectly illustrates God's clarion call to the Church today: "Come." Jesus is inviting us to step out of our comfortable religious boats and do something we have never done before. I am reminded of the law of inertia: An object in motion stays in motion and an object at rest stays at rest, until force is exerted. To some degree I believe the Church has functioned like an object at rest. We are waiting to see a move of God in our generation. We are wishing and hoping that God will "do it again." Dear friends, I believe that God is calling the Church to get off our "blessed assurance" and do something we have never done before. I believe that revival takes place when revived people take action.

The Miraculous Requires Risk

It is important that we understand the inextricable relationship between walking in the supernatural power of God and taking risks. By risk, I mean a mindset of stepping out in faith. By default, risk implies an exposure to danger or harm. The Kingdom of God, however, operates by a totally different economy. Faith is the currency of the Kingdom of God, and faith is often spelled R.I.S.K. Every time we desire to see God move in a way we have never seen before, it requires us to step out in faith. We must take the risk in order to see the manifestation. In other words, if you want to see what you have never seen before, you must be willing to do what you have never done before. In fact, the greater the risk, the greater the reward. God loves to meet us at the place where we abandoned our comfort zones. What do I mean by this?

I will never forget a testimony from a man in my church. He said that one day he was praying and asking God to partner with him to see miracles manifest in the life of someone in his sphere of influence. He said that as he prayed, he saw the face of a man standing on a particular street. By faith, he started walking down the street believing to see this man. As he walked, he stopped the first person that he saw, but the person was unreceptive. He thought that he had missed God. Yet there was an inner witness that he should keep walking. As he kept walking, he saw a man who resembled the man in his earlier vision, and he asked the man what was going on in his life. The man divulged that he was going through a very hard time. As he began ministering to the man, the power of God fell and the man accepted Jesus. Hallelujah! What would have happened if he had discounted the prompting of the Holy Spirit as his own random thoughts and stayed at home? That man might not have encountered God in the way he did and at the time he did. One of the keys to becoming a "Water Walker" is simply stepping out of the boat (i.e., your comfort zone). As I have said before, you will never walk on water if you never step out of the boat.

Overcoming the Fear of Failure

The truth is that every one of us faces the temptation to be afraid. In fact, fear is a normal part of life. Your body has a natural physiological response to danger or the unknown. It's called fight or flight. This is a form of self-preservation. But the Bible says that "God has not given us a spirit of fear, but of power and of love and of a sound mind" (2 Timothy 1:7). The word *fear* here is not referring to simple natural trepidation. This comes from the Greek word *deilia*, which means timidity, fearfulness or cowardice. Timidity is defined as a lack of courage or confidence. The truth is that you cannot operate in faith and timidity at the same time, because faith is confidence in the Word of God. We are to be full of faith, not full of fear.

Why do people have a fear of failure when it comes to spiritual things? Faith comes from what you are focused on. Fear, too, comes from what you are focused on. If we are focused on ourselves or the circumstances around us, it will produce timidity and fear. If we focus on the One who is calling us out of the boat, it produces courage and confidence. Why? Whom you listen to and what you look at determines what you believe. As long as Peter kept his eyes transfixed on Jesus, he had the supernatural boldness to walk on water, but the moment he took his eyes off Jesus was the moment he began to sink in fear. What are you focused on? Are you thinking about the embarrassment associated with "missing it"? Or are you focused on the joy associated with Jesus being glorified? What you focus on determines the posture of your heart, and your heart posture determines your level of confidence.

I will never forget the time I was praying for a woman who (at the time) had recently suffered a stroke. She had lost her ability to speak and the use of her right hand. Not only that, but this was being broadcast live to thousands of people. The first thought that came to my mind was, *If this woman doesn't get healed, then people will think I am a fraud!* That line of thinking didn't originate from God. I was focused on myself, not God or the well-being of the woman. After the Holy Spirit "checked" me, I repented and decided to step out. The only thing I thought to do was to take a big risk, so I put the microphone to her mouth and told her to shout, "Jesus!" The people with her became upset with me because they knew she was unable to speak. I told her again, "Say, 'Jesus!'" There was utter silence. Finally, I said again, "Say, 'Jesus!'" Suddenly, she grabbed the microphone with the hand she was supposedly unable to use and screamed, "J-J-J-Jesus!"

> **What you focus on determines the posture of your heart, and your heart posture determines your level of confidence.**

The church exploded in praise, and healings broke out. Glory to God! The only way to overcome fear is to step out in faith.

Action Activates Miracles

If you pay close attention, you will see that almost every miracle in the Bible is associated with a divine instruction that required a decisive action. For example, in the book of 2 Kings 5:10–14, there was a man known as Naaman who was a Syrian general who happened to also be a leper. He came to Elisha the prophet for healing, and Elisha instructed him to dip in the Jordan River. The Jordan River has historically been known as a dirty river. For this reason, Naaman was averse to engaging in such a humiliating activity. When he had finally had enough, he consented to follow the instructions of the man of God. The moment he obeyed the instruction was the moment he received his miracle. Oftentimes, acting on the Word of God is required in order to receive what God has promised you.

Another example of this is found in Matthew 12:13: "Then He said to the man, 'Stretch out your hand.' And he stretched it out, and it was restored as whole as the other." Notice that Jesus asked the man to stretch out his hand. He probably could have anointed his hand or physically touched him (as in other instances), but in this particular scenario, an instruction was given. When the man responded to the instruction, he received his miracle. Whether it is the action of the one ministering or the actions of the one receiving or both, there is no doubt that action activates miracles.

Another New Testament example is the account of the apostles Peter and John going to the temple in the book of Acts. They encountered a lame man who was asking for alms at the gate.

> When he saw Peter and John about to go into the temple grounds, he began asking to receive a charitable gift. But Peter, along with John, looked at him intently and said, "Look at us!" And he gave

them his attention, expecting to receive something from them. But Peter said, "I do not have silver and gold, but what I do have I give to you: In the name of Jesus Christ the Nazarene, walk!" And grasping him by the right hand, he raised him up; and immediately his feet and his ankles were strengthened. And leaping up, he stood and began to walk; and he entered the temple with them, walking and leaping and praising God. . . . But when Peter saw this, he replied to the people, ". . . On the basis of faith in His name, it is the name of Jesus which has strengthened this man whom you see and know; and the faith which comes through Him has given him this perfect health in the presence of you all.

Acts 3:3–8, 12, 16 NASB

He was told to fix his eyes on the apostles. He had to change something that he was doing in order to receive from God. I have said before, but I will say it again: To receive what you never had, you must do what you have never done. Glory to God!

The following are testimonies about faith in action shared by people who acted on the Word:

After being under Dr. Kynan's ministry for months, my husband and I were already seeing the manifestation of the favor of God over our lives through the power of revelation in Dr. Kynan's teaching. Every Sunday Dr. Kynan would preach about supernatural finances and we would sow in faith. One week in the summer of 2021, I took our kids to a children's conference. During this conference the pastor reiterated what we had already been learning about seedtime and harvest. On Wednesday of the weeklong conference, the Scripture that was read and broken down was the one about Jesus feeding the five thousand.

"Jesus replied, 'They do not need to go away. You give them something to eat.'

"'We have here only five loaves of bread and two fish,' they answered.

"'Bring them here to me,' he said. And he directed the people to sit down on the grass. Taking the five loaves and the two fish and looking up to heaven, he gave thanks and broke the loaves. Then he gave them to the disciples, and the disciples gave them to the people. They all ate and were satisfied, and the disciples picked up twelve basketfuls of broken pieces that were left over" (Matthew 14:16–20 NIV).

The pastor simply said, "Put it in the Master's hands, and let Him multiply it for you." In faith I did that. I sowed a seed of $200 dollars that week, and by Friday my husband called me and said his boss gave him a raise, but not just any raise—an annual raise of $36,000. I couldn't believe my ears. This could only be the Lord's doing, because it just didn't make sense. My husband had been working with the company for a year and half and was not expecting a raise at all. But because of the favor of God and the favor of man, the Lord provided. He is so faithful.

In 2020, I had a series of three divine encounters. . . . I saw evil altars—one in the Northeast, one in the Midwest, one over Louisiana, and one over Southern California. I then saw praying hands as we rose up and entered a courtroom. Jesus was sitting in the witness stand. He was light like in the Transfiguration.

The next divine encounter was July of 2020. As I was sleeping, a robe was placed on my back from behind. It was very heavy. So heavy it woke me up. To me it looked like the one in the picture in the hall at Joan Hunter's.

The third divine encounter was August 2020. I was sleeping and saw a white staircase suspended with a cord or rope on each corner like the blanket Peter saw. As I was watching the staircase, it began to rise up and was gone.

I read your book *Kingdom Authority* while we were in Teams classes, but I read it on my phone and quickly because we had several books to read. So two weeks ago I bought the book from the bookstore so I could really study it and write notes in it. On pages 120–122 I found the interpretation of my dreams. On page 120 is Revelation 1:5–6, where it says Jesus Christ is the faithful witness

. . . then in the next paragraph you begin, "Our understanding of the mantle of king and priest is . . . ," then you write, "Now we will take a deeper look at the role and responsibility of every believer to advance the kingdom of God as a king and a priest." Then on page 121 at the bottom: "Whereby we have the Divine right and supernatural endowment to make intercession for people, communities, and nations." So, we have the praying hands (intercession) Jesus as faithful witness, robe as mantle, and staircase moving up as advancing the Kingdom of God as king and priests.

When I put my son in daycare it was solely based on the price and what I calculated I could afford. I noticed things that didn't seem right, but I ignored them because the price of the daycare sold me. Several months later I had a very disturbing warning dream about my son; I woke up with a desire to pray specifically on his daycare. As I prayed I ask the Lord for a sign to know if I should take him out of that daycare. When I went to drop him off that morning I got my sign with his unusual behavior. I started looking for a new daycare that same day and I found one I really liked, but the price was double! But I took a step in faith and I said, "God, if this was You speaking to me, You will provide! My finances didn't change, nor bills, but shockingly I was able to pay everything with the new daycare! Several months later I got a discount and I'm now paying less then what the first daycare was. Shortly after that, I noticed his teacher started playing worship music in the mornings as the kids arrived! Not only did God supernaturally provide financially, but his teacher saturates the room with worship! I went from paying double (I feel like God was testing my faith), and I ended up paying less!

I hope you have been encouraged by these testimonies of people acting in their spiritual giftings, like words of knowledge. They took small steps of faith, obeying the nudge of the Holy Spirit, and they grabbed hold of the Word and the promises of God.

Faith without Works Is Dead

We have said before that "faith without works is dead" (James 2:20). Simply put, *faith* is an action word. There will be no miracles without corresponding action. Many people pray and ask God to do certain things or move in a certain way, but they do not follow up with corresponding action. James calls that "dead faith." The word *dead* comes from the Greek word *nekros*, which means destitute of life or inanimate. Miracles are a result of faith in action (we will explore this in more detail later).

To be honest with you, I am somewhat annoyed by the current climate of the so-called charismatic church. I do not believe that God has called us to be a community of people who have simply mastered certain spiritual buzzwords like "I am blessed and highly favored" or "I feel like God really wants to move!" It is time for us to pay the price. It is time for us to put our money where our mouth is, so to speak, and make sure that our profession of faith corresponds with our obedience.

Breaking the Spirit of Intimidation

Earlier, we talked about the tendency of many believers to fall prey to a spirit of intimidation. The Bible is clear that God has not given us a spirit of intimidation. So where does it come from? Intimidation and fear originate from the "father of lies," the devil. The word *intimidate* means to "frighten or overawe (someone), especially in order to make them do what one wants." The way the enemy accomplishes this is by telling you (especially through your thoughts) that you can't do something. Or if you do something (in obedience to the Word of God), that there will be a negative outcome.

You may be asking,

What if I pray for someone and they don't get healed?
What if I thought I was hearing from God but I wasn't?

What if that person doesn't respond positively to my attempt to share the Gospel?

What if that person doesn't receive my prophetic word?

All these thoughts and questions are meant to take the focus away from the most important thing: Jesus.

We can break the spirit of intimidation by asking empowering questions like

How can Jesus be glorified in this scenario?

How can this person experience God in a fresh way?

How can taking this risk strengthen my faith?

How can this supernatural encounter bring the person or people closer to God?

When you begin to ask the right questions, you disarm the devil. You back him into a corner and weaken his grip or your mind. And if you really want to give him a black eye, declare, "Greater is the One who lives in me than he who is in the world!" I declare that the power of Jesus is greater than the power of fear. Hallelujah!

SUMMARY QUESTIONS

1. Why does the miraculous require risk?
2. How can we overcome the fear of failure?
3. Why is it important to act on the Word?
4. What are questions to ask to break free from the spirit of intimidation?

MIRACLE ACTIVATION

Father, in the name of Jesus, I recognize that You speak and it comes to pass. Your Word never returns void; therefore, I can put my confidence and trust in Your Word. Help me fix my eyes on You and show me what I need to change in order to receive from You. I declare that actions activate miracles; therefore, I step out in obedience to the Word of God, and I receive the manifestation of answered prayer. I take risks according to Your Word and place a faith demand on everything that You have promised. Today I declare that I am stepping out from my comfort zone and into Your perfect will for my life, in the name of Jesus. Amen.

11

Possessing a Relentless Spirit

The Power of Perseverance

Do not cast away your confidence, which has great reward.

Hebrews 10:35

As I sat in the back of the classroom, my heart began to race as I thought about what I would have to face as soon as the bell rang. Moments earlier, I had engaged in an exchange of words with the biggest sixth grader in the entire school. As I sat and wondered whether I was talking to a student or an ex-convict, my adrenal glands went into overdrive as I prepared for the worst.

Suddenly, the bell rang.

As I walked out of the school toward the playground, there he was, this Goliath of a human being. I realized that I had insulted his mother during our earlier exchange, and I was probably about to pay for it now.

Before I could even think, he picked me up and threw me across the playground onto the dirt. At this point it felt like a scene from *Rocky 4*, and the Ivan Drago figure was standing over me with an intimidating visage. I could see my life flash before my eyes.

Then I heard an inner voice say, *Stand up and fight!*

In an instant, I rose to my feet and fought with every fiber of my being. With fists of fury, I threw every blow that was humanly possible until I was literally sitting on top of Goliath's shoulders, pounding his head like a pair of congas. In the twinkling of an eye, I realized I was winning. People began shouting my name as I rose triumphant.

The above story may seem like folklore or an anecdote, but I assure you it was very real when it happened. As a small kid, I was often incorporating a tremendous amount of sarcasm to keep the bullies at bay, but in this particular instance, it did not work, and I was forced to back up my words with actions. The one thing that I had to my advantage was a relentless fighting spirit. I never really backed down from a fight, even when I knew I would lose.

This attitude has been useful in my spiritual life. I apply the same logic to ministry and spiritual warfare. Never back down! Never give up or relent until you see the manifestation of God's promises.

What Is Your Battle Really Against?

I know that the focus of this book is the miraculous, but I would be remiss if I didn't address the elephant in the room: spiritual warfare. Walking in the miraculous power of God requires a sense of perseverance that few fully understand. The truth is, I didn't become an authority on the supernatural overnight. In fact, when my wife and I first started in ministry, I didn't really have a clue. There was much trial and error. Back then we didn't have schools of the miraculous to teach us these things. There were people I prayed for who didn't get healed. There were others I prayed for who died. Honestly, at times it was devastating.

Many people today treat miracles like a TikTok video—instant and entertaining. They omit the process that so many of us had to endure in order to gain a fuller understanding of the supernatural. There is an element of persistence necessary to see a sustained flow of the authentic power and presence of God in your life. There are also demonic forces that have been assigned to keep you trapped in fear and doubt. They work overtime to hinder you from moving into realms of God that you often dream about.

In chapter 10, I mentioned the spirit of intimidation and how there is a need to step out of the boat of fear and timidity. The truth is that the enemy works tirelessly to keep you in the boat. He wants to keep you frustrated and fearful. He wants you to live in a place called "What If?" He wants you to wonder if God can ever use you while never releasing your full potential. I am here to break you out of that prison of doubt and fear and invite you into a life of victory. This is not a physical battle, but a spiritual battle waged on the battlefield of the mind to impose limits on your life that God never ordained. Give the devil no place!

In this chapter, I endeavor to ask some of the most pervasive questions that come to your mind in an attempt to live your forward progress in the supernatural.

What If Nothing Happens?

Oftentimes, I hear the same question consistently: What if nothing happens? How many times have you prayed for someone and nothing happened? How many times have you expected God to do something and you did not see that prayer answered?

Jesus made a very profound statement in the gospel of John: "And whatever you ask in My name, that I will do, that the Father may be glorified in the Son. If you ask anything in My name, I will do it" (14:13–14). Notice that Jesus did not leave room for fear, doubt or trepidation. The statement is so important that He said it twice for emphasis: "If you ask anything in My name, I will do it." Do you believe that statement? There are two conditions:

1. *We must believe.* "Therefore I say to you, whatever things you ask when you pray, believe that you receive them, and you will have them" (Mark 11:24). The word *believe* comes from the Greek word *pisteuō*, which means to think to be true or to be persuaded. We must accept God's Word to be true and the final authority for all things pertaining to life.

2. *We must persevere.* "And He spoke a parable to them, that men always ought to pray and not lose heart" (Luke 18:1). We are admonished by our Lord to persevere in faith.

We will talk more about persistence a little later, but for now it is important to emphasize the importance of not giving up on God if something doesn't happen the first time. Don't quit; keep trying. If you pray for people and they don't see the manifestation of their healing, pray again. Don't be discouraged if you don't see something happen right away.

A Testimony of the Supernatural

Years ago, I heard a very powerful story of a woman who had a debilitating physical condition. Someone I knew had actually prayed for this woman. She was determined to receive healing from a severe deformity in her legs that rendered her completely crippled. She had suffered from this condition as long as she could remember. During a Healing School, she came up for prayer, and the leaders prayed over her. My friend went up to her and began declaring healing over her body. The woman even attempted to get up out of her wheelchair, but it did not turn out well. She ended up falling to the ground and suffering much embarrassment. She continued to believe God for her healing. Yet there was no physical manifestation. Several years later, when she was home alone on her birthday, she prayed a simple prayer: "Lord, if You would heal me, that would be the best birthday gift I could ever receive." Suddenly, her legs and feet begin to crack and twist. Her legs literally received strength. She jumped to her feet and walked across the room. When her husband came home from his errands, he saw his wife standing, and he fell to the ground and wept. Glory to God! Don't you dare give up on God if there is breath in your lungs. Keep believing!

Standing on the Word of God

I absolutely love my wife, Gloria. She is not only beautiful and kind, but she is also a woman of faith. In fact, she has taught me as much about faith as I have taught her. Many of you have heard me share this testimony, but I will share it again, because I believe it perfectly illustrates the power of perseverance.

When Gloria was pregnant with our first child, she had many complications, including diabetes. In an instant, God supernaturally healed her of diabetes. Unfortunately, there were other problems that contributed to a complicated delivery. My wife was in labor for over 24 hours with no dilation. The doctor came in and informed us that they would have to do an emergency C-section, but my wife was adamant against it. She told me that she would not have a C-section no matter what. Then, because she was so tired from the labor, she went to sleep.

At one point, the doctor said it was time to perform the surgery because the fetal heart rate was at risk of dropping. I begged the doctor to give us one hour, and she agreed under the condition that in exactly one hour they would proceed with the surgery.

I began to pray earnestly. I declared that my wife's cervix was dilated in the name of Jesus. I spoke to my daughter and told her to come out of that womb in the same way she went in. I prayed until I got really hungry, so I went to the cafeteria to get some chicken strips. When I returned to my wife's room, I began praying more.

After a few minutes, the nurse came in to prep my wife for surgery. I told her to check my wife one more time. As she checked my wife's cervix, she shouted, "Get the doctor, the baby's head is poking out!" I threw my chicken strips down, ran to my wife's aid and helped deliver my beautiful daughter. Glory to God!

The Lord said, *While your wife was giving birth to your physical daughter, I was teaching you how to birth the miraculous!* Hallelujah! We stood on the Word of God regardless of what the circumstances looked like.

Earlier, in chapter 9, we looked at the story of the woman with the issue of blood. Her story is our story in many ways, because she was willing to press through the crowd in order to receive her miracle. Her story is not just one of hope, but of perseverance. And there is a part of her story that many people miss. Why did she have so much confidence that if she touched Jesus, she would be made whole? As Western Christians reading the King James Bible, it may be easy for us to approach the text with our own presuppositions. When we read the story, there is an image of the woman grabbing Jesus' robe, but what if I told you there was more to the story than that?

"And besought him that they might only touch the hem of his garment: and as many as touched were made perfectly whole" (Matthew 14:36). The word used for *hem* here is the Greek word *kraspedon*, which actually means border, fringe or tassel. This is a significant part of the story. Why? God gave the Israelites very specific instructions:

"Speak to the children of Israel: Tell them to make tassels on the corners of their garments throughout their generations, and to put a blue thread in the tassels of the corners. And you shall have the tassel, that you may look upon it and remember all the commandments of the LORD and do them, and that you may not follow the harlotry to which your own heart and your own eyes are inclined."

Numbers 15:38–39

Jesus was probably wearing a tallit, but there is no doubt that as a Jewish man in the first century, He would have definitely adhered to the Torah by wearing the tassels on the borders of His garment, representing the law. This garment was also referred to as "wings" in Hebrew.

The story of the woman with the issue of blood was not just a story of a woman's individual faith, but it was a fulfillment of biblical prophecy in reference to the Messiah.

But to you who fear My name the Sun of Righteousness shall arise with healing in His wings; and you shall go out and grow fat like stall-fed calves.

Malachi 4:2

This woman understood that Jesus was the Messiah and that according to the prophet Malachi, the Messiah (the "Sun of Righteousness") would arise with healing in His (tassels), or wings. When she grabbed the borders of His garment, she was laying hold of the Word of God and the promise of healing. That is why Jesus turned to the woman and told her that her faith had made her whole. She stood on the Word of God and received the manifestation of God's promises.

Beloved, we must stand on the Word of God and receive the supernatural virtue that proceeds from the Sun of Righteousness.

Possessing a Relentless Spirit

Contrary to popular belief, walking in the supernatural power of God is not some passive exercise for the faint at heart. You must

> **Walking in the supernatural power of God is not some passive exercise for the faint at heart. You must possess a relentless spirit.**

possess a relentless spirit. What does it mean to be relentless? The word *relentless* is defined as "oppressively constant; incessant," "harsh or inflexible." On the surface these terms do not seem befitting of a Christian, but when applied to spiritual warfare or holding on to the promises of God, these terms are very appropriate.

In the gospel of Luke, chapter 18, we are told a story of a woman who sought vindication from an unjust judge. The Bible says,

> And he spake a parable unto them to this end, that men ought always to pray, and not to faint; saying, There was in a city a judge, which feared not God, neither regarded man: And there was a widow in that city; and she came unto him, saying, Avenge me of mine adversary. And he would not for a while: but afterward he said within himself, though I fear not God, nor regard man; yet because this widow *troubleth* me, I will avenge her, *lest by her continual coming she weary me.* And the Lord said, Hear what the unjust judge saith. And shall not God avenge his own elect, which cry day and night unto him, though he bear long with them? I tell you that he will avenge them speedily. Nevertheless when the Son of man cometh, shall he find faith on the earth?
>
> verses 1–8 KJV, emphasis added

Many of you reading this have read this parable before and we know that Jesus was talking about persevering in prayer, but I want to highlight some aspects of this story you may not have considered. Jesus used two very interesting words that the translators rendered "trouble." The first Greek word is *parechō*, which means to offer, and the second word is *kopos*, which means a beating. In other words, the unjust judge was saying that the woman keeps "reaching and beating" me with her request. She would not relent! Then the unjust judge says *this*: "lest by her continual coming she weary me." The Greek word here (translated as "weary") is actually *hypōpiazō*, which doesn't mean to make someone tired, but it actually means "to beat black and blue, to smite so as to cause bruises and livid spots." The word picture is that of a boxing match where the body of the boxer is beaten so badly that he is literally "worn out." The judge says, "I can't take any more of this metaphorical beating."

This story is not about the morality or kindness of the judge, but about the relentless persistence of the woman seeking vindication. This is not a picture of a passive person, but a determined warrior. The beauty of this story is the fact that God is actually omnibenevolent and longs to bless His children.

The Power of Receiving

One of the things I recognize in my many years of teaching on the supernatural is the sad reality that many people don't know how to receive from God. As I have mentioned before, receiving from God is not a passive exercise. I believe that many Christians are suffering from a low hermeneutical aptitude in regard to their understanding of the sovereignty of God. There are a large number of Christians who conflate the sovereignty of God with the passivity of man. They falsely assert that because God is sovereign, they have no part to play in God's plan and purpose for their lives. God will do it "if it is His holy will," many say. Nothing could be further from the truth!

The apostle John wrote in his gospel account, "And of His fullness we have all received, and grace for grace" (1:16). The word *received* here comes from the Greek word *lambanō*, which means to take or take with the hand or lay hold of something in order to use it. That doesn't seem passive to me. We must lay hold of the fullness of Jesus. We must appropriate the supernatural life we have been given in Christ. Receiving is not a passive action. Receiving is essentially possessing your possessions.

Imagine someone paying for some items at your favorite store. The person gives you the receipt and tells you that you only need to pick up your items at the layaway department. Would you sit there and wait for the items to drop in your lap? Would you stand there for hours staring at the customer service representative, waiting for them to know what is on your heart? Or would you walk boldly to the counter and tell them that you came to pick up your items? Why? Because even though someone else paid for the items, they belong to you. If you didn't have any proof of purchase or guarantee from your friend that the items were paid for and reserved in your name, it would be a totally different story.

Beloved, Jesus has paid a tremendous price to grant us a supernatural life in Him. His shed blood and the Holy Spirit are the evidence that this life belongs to us. Why would we sit and wait for God to give us what He has already given us in Christ? Our Friend Jesus has given us everything that pertains to life and godliness. He purchased this life for us in His own blood. The Word of God tells you exactly what is included in the package. We must receive what belongs to us.

Now imagine that the heir of a multibillion-dollar estate is given access to every penny of that estate. Everything has been willed to the child, and they are of the stipulated age to receive it. Would the child sit in a room in despair, hoping that one day he will be able to be blessed? In the world, people fight, kill and sue one another over earthly inheritances. We have a far greater inheritance. If miracles are our inheritance, then we ought to approach them as such. Heirs are not passive about their inheritance—they intentionally receive it with a sense of intentionality. Jesus died to give us a rich inheritance that far exceeds anything in this world. You can be insistent about this inheritance. The will is enforced when someone dies. Jesus died.

We must be possessive when walking in miracles. Your miracle belongs to you. It's yours—treat it like it's yours. You can pursue and be relentless without hesitation because it's already yours. Hallelujah!

SUMMARY QUESTIONS

1. Why should we possess a relentless spirit?
2. What's holding you back from ministering miracles?
3. What is the importance of receiving?
4. Why must we stand on the promises of God?

MIRACLE ACTIVATION

Father, in the name of Jesus, I thank You for Your overwhelming presence in my life. Thank You for giving me relentless persistence, like the woman with the issue of blood and the widow who sought vindication. You have called me to pray without ceasing; therefore, I declare that I possess a relentless spirit in matters of the Kingdom of God. I declare that I have a rich spiritual inheritance in Christ Jesus; therefore, I operate in the fulness of His Spirit. I declare that I stand on the promises of God. I declare that I am unmoved by the temporary circumstances and obstacles before me, but my heart is fixed, trusting in God. Today I press into the promises of God with boldness and audacity in the name of Jesus. Amen!

12

How to Maintain the Miraculous

Keeping a Heart Focused on Jesus

Show yourself in all respects to be a model of good works, and in your teaching show integrity, dignity, and sound speech that cannot be condemned, so that an opponent may be put to shame, having nothing evil to say about us.

Titus 2:7–8 ESV

In chapter 3, we discussed the importance of personal revival and the power of consecration in walking in the supernatural power of God. In today's climate of social media and instant gratification, the concept of purity seems to be antiquated and old-fashioned, but our character and private lifestyle are paramount when it comes to maintaining a lifestyle of the miraculous. I know that many claim that because God is gracious that He condones any behavior, but nothing could be further from the truth.

First of all, what is character? Character is "the mental and moral qualities distinctive to an individual." Old-fashioned folks would say that character is who you are when no one is looking. And why is it so important to have character, especially when it comes to miracles? How we live our lives privately and publicly determines how much of God's power we can be entrusted with.

In his gospel, John recounted how Jesus healed the man at the pool of Bethesda who had been crippled for 38 years. But there is a part to the story that we don't often talk about.

> Afterward Jesus found him in the temple, and said to him, "See, you have been made well. Sin no more, lest a worse thing come upon you."
>
> John 5:14

This man received a miracle by the mercy of God. It had nothing to do with his faith or his lifestyle, but Jesus told him to "sin no more, lest a worse thing come upon you." His personal character and lifestyle played a vital part in his miracle maintenance.

Character Matters

I want you to imagine that someone bought you a $600,000 Rolls-Royce and took care of all the taxes; the only thing you were responsible for was the maintenance of the vehicle. You had to make sure you got the oil changes and tire rotations and any other regularly required service. One day the engine light comes on, but instead of you taking it into the service center, you go another 30,000 miles without service. What would happen? Your vehicle would break down. Why? Your refusal to maintain the vehicle would compromise the engine and other vital components, and the car would not function according to its original design.

The same is true of our spiritual lives. We have received salvation and a supernatural life, along with the grace (unmerited favor) of God, but we are commanded to "walk circumspectly" (Ephesians 5:15). When we refuse to live within the confines of God's Word and we neglect regular spiritual disciplines that are required to live a healthy spiritual life, the moral and spiritual fabric of our lives will begin to break down. This is what some call "burnout."

After many years of pastoring, I look back and realize that many pastors I know are no longer in ministry today. Many of them were gifted preachers, teachers and prophets. They could preach the paint off the walls and tell you what you ate for breakfast two years ago, but their personal spiritual lives lacked discipline and "regular maintenance." They were like that $600,000 Rolls-Royce broken down on the side of the road. It is beautiful to look at, but it is not functional.

Friends, God is not simply interested in what you do for Him or what you receive from Him. He is interested in who you are. In fact, the greatest miracle is a life conformed to the image of Jesus.

How to Maintain a Healthy Spiritual Life

I want to share five things that I believe are vital in maintaining a healthy spiritual life that will foster and increase the manifestation of the authentic supernatural power of God.

1. The Word

It is amazing to me that many people want the supernatural, but they don't have a love for the Word of God. Jesus is the Word, and to love Jesus is to love His Word and desire to meditate in and obey it. You will discover that the more you study the Word, the more you will position yourself to hear God's voice clearly, and the more you hear His Word, the more your faith for miracles will grow. As a result of a firm foundation in the Word of God, you will begin to have more sustainable supernatural encounters. God does not give us encounters so that we can simply feel good, but He manifests Himself to us miraculously so that we can experience His love more deeply—so that we can come into a greater understanding of who He is.

Earlier, in chapter 3, we talked about biblical meditation as opposed to New Age meditation. I believe that one of the most powerful tools that enables us to tap into a sustained flow of miracles is meditating on the Word of God. How do we do this?

- Write down Scriptures that are related to specific areas in the supernatural (e.g., prayer, prophecy, dreams, visions, angels, etc.).
- Meditate on those Scriptures throughout the day in addition to your regular Bible reading.
- Begin to thank God for a greater manifestation of His presence in those areas of your life. Maybe you desire a more active dream life, or you want to feel God's presence more.
- Find biblically based teaching on those specific areas.
- Speak those Scriptures out loud as often as you possibly can.

The Word of God grounds our spiritual experiences and acts as a litmus test that gauges the authenticity and purity of those experiences. Even God is governed by His Word.

I will worship toward Your holy temple, and praise Your name for Your lovingkindness and Your truth; for You have magnified Your word above all Your name.

Psalm 138:2

The Bible also says,

In the beginning was the Word, and the Word was with God, and the Word was God.

John 1:1

If God acknowledges His own Word as the final authority for everything in the cosmos, how much more highly should we regard the Word of God as the final authority for our lives? People who don't have a deep reverence for the Word of God open their spiritual lives to a spirit of deception. This is why many people have unstable lives in the name of spirituality. They attend every conference known to man, but they don't bear lasting spiritual fruit (we will touch on this in the next section). Pray that God will give you a hunger and love for His Word that will usher you into deeper devotion in your spiritual life and open the door to greater expressions of His power and love.

2. *Spiritual Community*

God loves His Church, and contrary to popular belief, community is a vital part of our spiritual growth and development. Godly community is a catalyst to walk in the supernatural power of God. The word *community* means a group of people living in the same place or having a particular characteristic in common. Community creates an environment of common interest and support. The Body of Christ is a spiritual community that Christ established, which He actually commands us to be connected to.

The reason why spiritual community is such a vital part of walking in the supernatural is because each member of the community supplies a necessary component that we cannot receive while disconnected from the community. Imagine a physical body: Every part of the body plays a vital role in the health and well-being of the body as a whole.

There are four aspects of spiritual community that I want to highlight:

- *Fellowship.* We are called to fellowship with one another. The word fellowship comes from the Greek word *koinōnia*, which means "fellowship, association, community, communion, joint participation, intercourse." It carries with it the connotation of intimacy. God has called us to intimacy with Himself and with one another.

- *Accountability.* The word *accountability* can be defined as "the fact or condition of being accountable; responsibility." Someone held accountable is "required or expected to justify actions or decisions." When we are accountable, we are answerable to someone else other than ourselves. Having to give an account for our decisions causes us to give more consideration to what we do and say, both privately and publicly. I believe this is important, because a healthy spiritual life is one of biblical discipleship—and discipleship involves accountability.

- *Encouragement.* The Church is a living organism composed of imperfect people passionately pursuing and being pursued by a perfect Savior. Community affords us the opportunity to encourage one another. So, as believers, let's "consider one another in order to stir up love and good works" (Hebrews 10:24).

- *Communication.* The passage in Hebrews continues by saying, "Not forsaking the assembling of ourselves together, as is the manner of some, but exhorting one another, and so much the more as you see the Day approaching." Within the word *community* is the word *communication.* When we engage in spiritual community, we can ask each other questions, share our experiences and learn from one another.

The Bible says, "Two are better than one, because they have a good reward for their labor. For if they fall, one will lift up his companion. But woe to him who is alone when he falls, for he has no one to help him up" (Ecclesiastes 4:9–10). Spiritual community provides mutual encouragement, along with fellowship, accountability and communication.

3. *Worship*

It is my firm conviction that true worship is a vital component to maintaining a miraculous lifestyle. When we worship God in Spirit and in truth, we are constantly inviting His presence into our lives. Bill Johnson once said that the Holy Spirit is in every believer, but He does not rest upon every believer.[1] I believe this is absolutely true. We must develop a love and reference for the presence of God if we want to live in the miraculous daily. His presence is miraculous. The more you learn to get in His presence, the more you will learn to sense His presence, and the more you learn to sense His presence, the more you will experience His presence.

Worship is not a series of slow songs at church. It is not dim lights and smoke machines (I can only imagine the expression on the face of the early Christian patriarchs as they look down from heaven on us), but worship is a lifestyle of constantly acknowledging the Holy Spirit and yielding in submission and partnership with Him. Think of the miraculous not as something God does, but as something you release. Worship is our conscious awareness of the indwelling presence of God as well as His manifest presence upon our lives. We often hear the expression "living in the secret place," but that is a very real place—where we abide in the space of constant fellowship and communion with God. Worship focuses our hearts on Jesus and not on ourselves. This is critical in the life of every born-again believer. Unfortunately, we live in a society where people want to rush everything, including God, but we must learn to wait in His presence.

> **Worship is a lifestyle of constantly acknowledging the Holy Spirit and yielding in submission and partnership with Him.**

One day in a service, I began to just wait in His presence. The glory of God filled the room. The Holy Spirit began to move powerfully. You could sense and feel the shift in the atmosphere. All of a sudden, I began to topple under the weight of His presence, and my ushers had to catch me on the stage. Apparently, while I was on the floor, the Holy Spirit began to do a deep "surgical work" in the hearts of His people. People began weeping as they were set free from all types of oppression and bondage. Glory to God! True worship is a weapon in our spiritual arsenal.

4. Gratitude

One of the most neglected spiritual principles when it comes to walking in the supernatural is the power of gratitude (I also call this the Law of Gratitude). What is gratitude, and why is it so important? Gratitude is defined as "the quality of being thankful; readiness to show appreciation for and to return kindness." Simply put, gratitude is being thankful. I often tell people that what we appreciate "appreciates" (as in increases in value).

A perfect example of this is the story of the ten lepers.

> Now it happened as He went to Jerusalem that He passed through the midst of Samaria and Galilee. Then as He entered a certain village, there met Him ten men who were lepers, who stood afar off. And they lifted up their voices and said, "Jesus, Master, have mercy on us!"
>
> So when He saw them, He said to them, "Go, show yourselves to the priests." And so it was that as they went, they were cleansed.
>
> And one of them, when he saw that he was healed, returned, and with a loud voice glorified God, and fell down on his face at His feet, giving Him thanks. And he was a Samaritan.
>
> So Jesus answered and said, "Were there not ten cleansed? But where are the nine? Were there not any found who returned to give glory to God except this foreigner?" And He said to him, "Arise, go your way. Your faith has made you well."
>
> Luke 17:11–19

Notice that the Samaritan (someone who was ill favored by the Jewish community) was the only person who returned to give thanks, and his miracle was upgraded from being healed of leprosy to being made totally whole. Leprosy was degenerative, and oftentimes lepers would lose fingers and other extremities. The nine lepers were cleansed of their leprosy, but they still probably had missing fingers, but the Samaritan was totally restored. Why? Because of the power of gratitude.

We live in a culture that is riddled with ingratitude. I once bought fresh food for a homeless person, and he said to me, "I don't like this kind of burger!" By all means, everyone has a right to have a preference, but the tone in which it was spoken was very ungrateful. We must learn to celebrate everything that God does for us. The more you give God glory, the more He will manifest His glory. Did you catch what I just said?

Maybe you haven't led a crusade of a million people, but you shared your faith with your co-worker, and he or she came to faith in Jesus. Treat that one like one million. The more gratitude you show for every supernatural experience, the more God will increase them. Maybe you are believing in God for a financial miracle—you need $50,000—but God blessed you with $5. Praise Him for the $5 like it's $50,000, and it'll be just a matter of time before you receive the $50,000. This is just an example, and here's another one.

Years ago, when we first started our church, we were meeting in our living room. I can remember one of our first services. There were about five people, including my immediate family, at the time. I was very frustrated because I thought I was going to have a megachurch the first day I started. The Lord asked me a question in my frustration. He said, *Son, if this is all I give you, will you still be faithful to Me?* Honestly, I didn't answer immediately because I knew that God could read my heart. But after giving it some thought, I said, "Yes, Lord! If all You gave me was five people, I would still serve You faithfully. Thank You, Lord!" About fifteen minutes later, there was an unexpected knock on the door. When I opened the door, there was a group of people standing there. They

Your gratitude is a seed for your next harvest of miracles.

asked, "Is there a church service going in here?" I said, "Yes," and they came in and we had church. It's safe to say that we have more than five members today. As I think about that story, I'm grateful that God didn't give me the megachurch right away, because I was not ready to handle that kind of increase.

Over time, God has taught me the supernatural power of gratitude. With every blessing and miracle, I have learned to give God praise. The more I praise Him for the little things, the more they grow. Your gratitude is a seed for your next harvest of miracles. Glory to God!

5. *Your Testimony*

The Bible says, "They overcame him by the blood of the Lamb and by the word of their testimony, and they did not love their lives to the death" (Revelation 12:11). I firmly believe that our testimony ignites our faith for more miracles. Whenever we hear a testimony or share our testimony, it stirs up something in the hearts of the hearers. This is why it is so important to share our testimony whenever God does something for us. No matter how apparently small the testimony seems to be, sharing what God does for us is a prophetic act that ignites a greater desire for the miraculous power of God. Never underestimate the power of your testimony.

I can remember something that happened during one of our camp meetings. As I was preaching, the Lord told me to sow financially into one of the young men who was in attendance. I didn't know who he was. The Lord just told me to give him a certain amount. I have done things like this many times, but the person would just say thank-you and go on about their business. This gentleman, however, was intentional about standing up the next day and coming forward to give his testimony. With tears in his eyes, he shared how God had met a serious financial need the previous day. As he was testifying, the Lord told me to give him a double portion. So I doubled the offering from the previous day. As I told him that God told me to sow into him again, tears filled his eyes and he fell to the ground. As he was on the ground, God told several people to sow large financial gifts into his life.

As you can see, there is power in your testimony. Don't allow the enemy to talk you out of sharing it. This is how you silence the mouth of the accuser of the brethren. Tell your story! Tell people what God has done for you. Share with people what God delivered you from.

What are you expecting from God today? Thank Him in advance. Find a reason to give God glory for every single thing you can think of, and if you run out of things to thank Him for, just thank Him for the breath in your lungs.

SUMMARY QUESTIONS

1. Why does character matter in maintaining the miraculous?
2. How can you avoid opening yourself to the spirit of deception?
3. What is the Law of Gratitude?
4. What grounds our spiritual experiences and acts as a litmus test that gauges the authenticity and purity of those experiences?

MIRACLE ACTIVATION

Father, I thank You for the integrity and authority of Your Word. Your Word is the final authority in my life, and it is the foundation for all things that pertain to life and godliness. I believe that the greatest miracle in my life is the work You are doing in me to conform me to the image of Your Son, Jesus. I declare that my heart is focused on the Miracle Worker (Jesus), and as a result, His miraculous power flows through my life in the name of Jesus. I declare that my life is shielded from the spirit of deception and that I delight in the Word of God daily. I declare that I possess a spirit of gratitude, and the Law of Gratitude opens doors to greater manifestations of the power and presence of God in my life. In the name of Jesus, I pray. Amen.

13

Ready, Set, Go

Practical Steps in the Miraculous

And He said to them, "Go into all the world and preach the gospel to every creature."

Mark 16:15

So far, you have received many keys to activating and walking in the supernatural power of God. As mentioned, action activates miracles. This is a recurring theme in this book and in my teaching on the supernatural in general. In this chapter, we will review some previous material that we have discussed, but also give you some practical steps to walking in the miraculous that every believer should know.

In the gospel of Mark, Jesus made a very profound statement. He said, "Go ye into all the world, and preach the gospel to every creature" (16:15 KJV). Then He said in verses 17–18,

"And these signs will follow those who believe: In My name they will cast out demons; they will speak with new tongues; they will take up serpents; and if they drink anything deadly, it will by no means hurt them; they will lay hands on the sick, and they will recover."

First, I want to look at the previous statement, "Go ye . . ." The word *go* comes from the Greek word *poreuō*, which means to transfer. The root word is *peira*, which means a trial, experience or attempt. Jesus transferred power and authority to His disciples and sent them out to experience what He put inside them. This commissioning was not just relegated to the first-century apostles, but in a sense, this was a commissioning to the global Church throughout the ages. As believers, all of us are called to release the Kingdom. We all have been given the power of the Holy Spirit and the spiritual authority to move in the miraculous power of God. How else will the world know the reality of heaven?

The miraculous is easy. Jesus already did the heavy lifting. We simply need to yield to the Holy Spirit and step out in His power and authority.

I know that there is some fuzzy-faced theologian pulling on his bow tie, shouting, "Blasphemy!," but I can assure you, by the whole counsel of Scripture and the record of Church history, that God didn't go to sleep after the death of the first-century apostles. The notion that miracles are for today is far from blasphemous; it is totally biblical. The God of Abraham, Isaac and Jacob is transgenerational, and His power knows no bounds. I'm going to make a statement that seems unrealistic, but I'm going to make the statement anyway: The miraculous is easy. Jesus already did the heavy lifting. We simply need to yield to the Holy Spirit and step out in His power and authority.

The ABCs of Miracles

Just as children must learn to stand before they can walk, and students must learn their ABCs before they can write, you must understand the rudimentary truths of the Word that will create a solid framework from which you will be able to operate in the miraculous. That is why I have endeavored to make this book very simple and easy to understand. Once you learn the ABCs of walking in the miraculous, you will realize how simple it really is. Let me share these ABCs with you.

Availability

Growing up, there was a song that I would hear in church called "I'm Available to You" that talked about emptying our wills to God and being a vessel that's totally surrendered for His use.[1] One of the most foundational requirements for walking in the supernatural is availability. The *Oxford Dictionary* defines *availability* as "the quality of being able to be used or obtained; the state of being otherwise unoccupied; freedom to do something." When we are available, our time and agenda are unoccupied when it comes to our relationship with God. It is an attitude that says, *Lord, whatever You desire to do, I am willing!*

Too many Christians today have schedules that are too full. Please don't misunderstand me; I know there are many responsibilities and obligations that we must attend to, but there is a pervasive attitude in the Church today that demands that God moves on our terms and on our time schedule. The average church service is an hour long from start to finish. It takes longer than an hour to get your car detailed, your nails manicured, your oil changed, your hair cut or to wait in line at a popular restaurant, yet we want to put stipulations on the most important person on earth: the Holy Spirit.

A revolutionary aspect of growing in the supernatural is relinquishing control of your agenda. In fact, this is actually a requirement for every believer. We must be willing to yield our time, talents and treasures to God daily. The Bible says this:

> I beseech you therefore, brethren, by the mercies of God, that ye present your bodies a living sacrifice, holy, acceptable unto God, which is your reasonable service. And be not conformed to this world: but be ye transformed by the renewing of your mind, that ye may prove what is that good, and acceptable, and perfect, will of God. For I say, through the grace given unto me, to every man that is among you, not to think of himself more highly than he ought to think; but to think soberly, according as God hath dealt to every man the measure of faith.
>
> Romans 12:1–3 KJV

We are commanded to present our bodies (and our lives) as living sacrifices to God. Paul, the writer of the epistle to the church in Rome, called it "your reasonable service" (verse 1). Another way of saying this is "That is the least you can do." I am sorry to tell you, but you are not doing God a favor by attending church or reading your Bible. "It is the least you can do" as one who has been redeemed. In fact, I would argue that we are doing ourselves a favor by practicing those spiritual disciplines. I believe, as Paul asserted in the passage above, we must be transformed by the renewing of our minds. We must change the way we think if we want to experience God on a deeper level. We must remember that we are the clay, and He is the Potter; He is the Creator, and we are the creation.

In an age of narcissism and self-aggrandizement, it is easy to fall into the trap of believing that everything revolves around our preferences; it does not. We must have an attitude of availability, asking, "Lord, what do You want to do today?" Ask God how He desires to partner with you to release the Kingdom of God. When you go to the grocery store say, "Lord, who do You want to save and heal in here today?" This breaks the grip of self-consciousness and puts the focus back on God as the Source of faith and boldness.

When we make ourselves available to God, we position ourselves for every opportunity to experience the supernatural. I believe that God is waiting on our "Yes!"

Belief

As mentioned several times in this book, faith is the currency of the Kingdom of heaven. Our faith in God is foundational to walking in the supernatural. Why? If you don't believe that God is exactly who He says He is, you will never take a risk and step out to see His power manifest. Belief is defined as an acceptance that a statement is true or that something exists. What we accept as true determines what we believe, and what we believe determines our actions.

One of the biggest issues in the Church today besides biblical illiteracy is the spiritual cognitive dissonance evidenced by the lack of power and the lack of consistency with the songs we sing on Sunday and the lifestyle we live Monday through Saturday. For instance, we say, "I surrender all!" on Sunday, but when God asks us to do something we don't understand or make a sacrifice that we did not budget for, we tend to express reluctance. Why? Because we don't always believe what we say we believe. This is not a point to be discouraged about; it is an area of opportunity. We must challenge ourselves in this area.

In Romans 1:16 the apostle Paul wrote, "For I am not ashamed of the gospel of Christ, for it is the power of God to salvation for everyone who believes, for the Jew first and also for the Greek." Notice the condition: "for everyone who believes." In other words, the *dynamis* power of God contained within the Gospel of Jesus Christ is activated by believing. Simply put, we must believe. The Israelites in the Old Testament didn't enter into the Promised Land because of their unbelief. We must mix our faith with the Word of God and respond accordingly.

The gospel of Matthew describes how Jesus left the home of a ruler where He had just performed a miracle, and "two blind men followed Him, crying out and saying, 'Son of David, have mercy on us!'" (9:27). In the next verse, Jesus asked the blind men a profound question: "Do you believe that I am able to do this?" Their response was simple yet powerful: "Yes, Lord." In response to their profession of faith, Jesus touched their eyes, and they were completely healed. Glory to God! I believe that Jesus is asking the Church that same question today: Do we really believe that He is able to do this? If the answer is yes, then the only appropriate response is to act in faith and allow God to manifest His power. If the answer is no, then we must challenge ourselves to go deeper.

Compassion

The life of Jesus is the archetype and blueprint for a life of miracles. As we said before, if we want to understand what God thinks about miracles, we need only look at Jesus. He is the ultimate example for every believer. He is the standard. What was the ethos of Jesus' earthly ministry? "When Jesus went out He saw a great multitude; and He was moved with *compassion* for them, and healed their sick" (Matthew 14:14, emphasis added). Jesus' ministry was characterized by compassion and a deep love for humanity. The word *compassion* is defined as "sympathetic pity and concern for the sufferings or misfortunes of others." In the original Greek, this is a much stronger word. It comes from the Greek word *splagchnizomai*: "to be moved as to one's bowels, hence to be moved with compassion, have compassion (for the bowels were thought to be the seat of love and pity)"; the root literally means intestines. Jesus was moved so deeply by the pain of others that He could feel it in His bowels. In other words, He was affected so much by the suffering of others that it compelled Him to action. Whenever Jesus was moved by compassion, He did something supernatural (either prayed, taught or performed miracles).

This theme is mentioned several times in the gospels and epistles. The Bible says, "For we do not have a High Priest who cannot sympathize with our weaknesses, but was in all points tempted as we are, yet without sin" (Hebrews 4:15). Jesus is our Great High

Priest, who is aware and sympathetic toward every weakness and temptation we face. Why? Because He has been there, done that and "got the T-shirt" (as they say). He experienced every aspect of humanity, yet without sin. There is something about compassion (the ability to empathize with the pain of others) that releases miracles. Sometimes when I minister to people, I feel their pain and begin to weep. Every time I do this, I sense a strong anointing for healing come over me and the person I am praying with, and in most cases, there is some physical manifestation of healing or breakthrough.

I will never forget an experience when I was praying for a man in church who looked very frightening. He was one of the largest human beings I have ever seen in my life. He was probably six feet five (at least), had solid muscle and looked like a character from a superhero comic book. Aside from his rough appearance, his visage was very aggressive and intimidating. If I can be honest, I was a bit intimidated to pray for this man, but I obeyed the unction of the Spirit and prayed anyway. As I prayed for him, the Holy Spirit prompted me to tell him that God loved him. As I spoke those words, the presence of God came upon him. I sensed such a love for him. I reached up and pulled this big man into my chest and held him as if I were holding my own son. Suddenly, he started wailing and weeping. He was set free from bondage. Glory to God! We must learn to operate in compassion as Jesus does, and by so doing, release the miraculous power of God.

Think of compassion as a sort of superpower. Whenever a superpower is activated—the superhero is no longer functioning as a mere mortal, but he or she is tapped into something supernatural—it changes everything. Compassion will change the way you pray, minister and interact with others. Give it a try!

How to Minister in the Miraculous

Now that we have provided the ABCs of supernatural ministry, I want to teach you how to minister in the miraculous effectively. It doesn't matter whether you are a pastor, police officer or politician (or anything in between), these practical keys will help you to activate and release the supernatural power of God and minister to the people around you.

1. Have the right mindset/attitude.

The first thing we must have in order to minister in the miraculous is a right mindset and positive mental attitude. We must understand that the goal of supernatural ministry is the advancement of the Kingdom of God and the establishment of the reality of heaven in the hearts of the people to whom we minister. Simply put, it is not about us. We are never to focus on ourselves.

Earlier, I introduced the concept of partnering with God to manifest His power and presence. For some of you, this may seem like a strange concept. *How can I partner with God?* you might ask. To others this may serve as a reminder that you and I have a part to play in God's agenda on the earth. Nevertheless, our mentality must be based on the truth that He is God and we are His ambassadors. As an ambassador, I am a representative of heaven. Every person I pray for (or with) and every situation that presents itself is an assignment from heaven. Every encounter is an opportunity to bring God glory.

> **You don't get what you deserve. You get what you expect.**

We must have an optimistic attitude when ministering. As I mentioned earlier, every time I pray for someone or minister to someone, I always expect something good to happen. In chapter 9, I said that you don't get what you deserve. You get what you expect. Our attitude affects what we expect and how much we expect from God. As it relates to the supernatural, your attitude determines your altitude. If you want to see greater, think bigger. Do not allow fear or discouragement to limit your thinking. Meditate on the Word of God in order to build a victorious mindset.

2. Ask the right questions.

In chapter 10, I spoke about the need to ask empowering questions in the context of breaking the spirit of intimidation. And here I want to highlight again the importance of asking empowering questions as opposed to disempowering questions. For example, "What if they don't get healed?" is a disempowering question. In life, I have discovered the power of asking the right questions.

In the gospel of John, Jesus asked an empowering question. When He saw a crippled man lying next to the pool of Bethesda, "and knew that he already had been in that condition a long time, He said to him, 'Do you want to be made well?'" (5:6). The man had been there for 38 years (that is a long time), and his morale was totally crippled by discouragement and despair. I believe that Jesus was giving us a pattern for supernatural ministry.

I believe that breakthroughs and miracles are provoked by asking yourself the right questions.

What will it take for my life to change?
How many people will be impacted by my obedience to
   God?
What is God asking of me right now?
What do I need to confront in my own thinking to overcome
   the doubt and unbelief that I face?

Along with asking ourselves empowering questions, we must also learn how to ask empowering questions to the people we are ministering to. For example,

- In what areas of your life do you need to encounter God?
- How can I pray for you?
- What do you need God to do for you today?
- Will you be made whole?

- Do you believe that Jesus can heal you?
- How did you feel after I prayed for you?

You can also ask yourself insightful questions that will enable you to make necessary changes to the way you pray or approach circumstances.

What is hindering this prayer from being answered?
Are there areas of disobedience in my life that are keeping me stuck in a certain place?
How do I address these areas?
Am I approaching this the right way?
What is the right way to approach this problem or difficulty?

In chapter 11, I talked about my encounter during the Healing School. I prayed for people to get healed of certain ailments, and nothing happened. This prompted me to ask the Holy Spirit, *What is going on?* He told me I was praying for the wrong things. I then realized (by revelation) that I was supposed to focus on unforgiveness, bitterness and offense. When I made the necessary change, many people were healed.

3. Follow up.

We spoke earlier about the importance of persistence in the supernatural. If you want to walk in the supernatural power of God consistently, you must learn the importance of follow-up. Just as Moses turned aside to inquire about the burning bush, we must be willing to pursue or investigate something further. When we pray for people or minister to people, there is nothing wrong with following up to gain an understanding of the impact of that prayer or words spoken over that person.

One thing about me is that I ask a lot of questions. I often ask people, "What did you get from that message?," "What did God show you when I was praying for you?," "How did that make you feel?" or any other question I can think of at the time. Just like a second and third visit to the doctor are important when receiving care, following up with the people you are ministering to is important. Follow-up gives you greater insight and clarity into how God is working through you and what He is doing, and it lets people know you are genuinely concerned with their spiritual lives. Remember, the goal is not my own personal satisfaction, but the healing and restoration of the person you are ministering to so that God can be glorified and the person can be benefited.

4. Don't be afraid to pray again.

People often ask me, "What if I pray for someone and nothing happens?" The answer is very simple. "Pray again!" Don't be afraid to pray again. I can remember praying for healing in someone's back, and after I prayed, the person still felt the pain. I simply asked, "How does it feel now?," then proceeded to pray again. Healing may happen the first time, or it may take several times to see the manifestation.

> Then He came to Bethsaida; and they brought a blind man to Him, and begged Him to touch him. So He took the blind man by the hand and led him out of the town. And when He had spit on his eyes and put His hands on him, He asked him if he saw anything.
> And he looked up and said, "I see men like trees, walking."
> Then He put His hands on his eyes again and made him look up. And he was restored and saw everyone clearly.
>
> Mark 8:22–25

All of us can be encouraged by the fact that even Jesus prayed for someone more than once. Did you hear what I said? Even our Lord was unafraid to pray more than once in order to get the desired outcome. Keep praying. Keep pressing in! This builds your faith, hope and confidence in God. Persistent prayer also communicates to the people you are praying for that you are more interested in their healing and well-being than in your own ego.

In conclusion, we must confront the lies that keep us bound in cycles of fear and intimidation. Sometimes you have to make a faith declaration that doesn't agree with your feelings. You must give God a yes by faith. Unfortunately, we live in such a climate of intellectualism in the Western world that there is a tendency for people to overanalyze God's Word. This leads to the "paralysis of analysis." God wants you to get out of your "thinker" and get into your "knower." We need a divine reset that will override fear and cause us to move to a place of faith and trust in God. Just believe. Just receive. Just do it!

SUMMARY QUESTIONS

1. Why is it important to ask the right questions?
2. What are the correct attitudes and mindsets to approach miracles?
3. Why should we follow up after praying for others?
4. Why is it important for us to have belief when ministering miracles?

MIRACLE ACTIVATION

Father, in the name of Jesus, I am thankful for Your abiding presence in and upon my life. Thank You for the boldness to step out in faith and experience Your miraculous power. Today, I declare that I have an attitude of expectancy and look forward to supernatural encounters with Your Spirit daily. I make myself available to You completely; do whatever You desire to do in and through me. I yield to the Holy

Spirit and step out in Your power and authority. Father, I am ready to go forth in Your power and purpose and transform the world around me through Your glorious presence. Today, I declare that I am a "Water Walker" and my life will never be the same. Nothing is impossible to me because I hear, believe and act upon Your Word daily in the name of Jesus. I am a world changer! In Jesus' name, Amen.

14

Heroes in the Miraculous

We Didn't Get Here on Our Own

Therefore we also, since we are surrounded by so great a cloud of witnesses, let us lay aside every weight, and the sin which so easily ensnares us, and let us run with endurance the race that is set before us.

Hebrews 12:1

Throughout this book, I have endeavored to lay a solid foundation for every believer who desires to release miracles—every day. This message represents over thirty years of ministry and experiences that have radically transformed my life. People often say that the advantage of a mentor is the benefit of their experiences without the pain of their process. But I did not get where I am on my own. Many awesome men and women of God have gone before me who laid the foundation that I am standing on. I and so many others are standing on the shoulders of giants. In this final chapter, I want to take this opportunity to acknowledge the great generals, both past and present, who have helped to shape me into the person I am today (through their writings, teachings or direct relationship).

Maria Woodworth-Etter

Maria Woodworth-Etter (1844–1924) was an uneducated, painfully timid woman who was isolated much of the time, sickly and poor. Considering that women were silenced by culture and the Church—not being allowed to speak or teach publicly, not allowed in the pulpit and not allowed to vote—the mountain of circumstances against her presented reason enough for silence, but the struggle continued. She didn't know how she could go into ministry. She was terrified with fear of talking before people. Her husband disallowed it, and her oldest daughter was also against it. To further complicate matters, she had small children.

In your wildest imagination, you wouldn't see Woodworth-Etter as an instrument of God who would dispense His love and mercies to generations, changing the lives of hundreds of thousands through her call to evangelism and the inspiring books she wrote. I am most impacted by the fact that she was a dynamic preacher during a time when women were not allowed to preach, and yet she preached with such tenacity and boldness. Despite the fact that she lost five of her six children, she released her faith in the power of God, and as a result many were saved, healed and delivered from the power of darkness.

Aimee Semple McPherson

Aimee Semple McPherson (1890–1944) is perhaps best known as the founder of the Foursquare Gospel Church.

As a female preacher and something of a Pentecostal novelty, Aimee Semple McPherson . . . [delivered] faith-healing demonstrations in which crutches were tossed aside and the blind were made to see. By 1922, she was breaking attendance records set by the biggest evangelical names at the time, such as Billy Sunday, the former baseball star. In San Diego, more than 30,000 people turned out for one of her events, and the Marines had to be called in for crowd control. There, McPherson laid hands on a supposedly paralyzed woman who rose from her chair and walked. The audience reached a frenzy.

The constant travel began to take its toll, and McPherson decided to settle down in Los Angeles, where she raised funds to build the Angelus Temple in Echo Park. She packed the 5,300-capacity building in services held seven days a week. Her style was light-hearted and whimsical at times, yet she spoke and sang with power and passion.[1]

McPherson had become a household name in the United States by 1926 and continued to pastor and grow her church until her death in 1944. "The Foursquare Gospel Church was worth millions at the time, and today claims nearly 9 million members worldwide."[2]

I will never forget preaching at a Four Square church in Australia. It was a very small church, and the pastor had been over the church for 25 years. As I sat back and pondered about the church, I was reminded that this church existed because of the pioneering spirit of a woman that society deemed unfit to preach because of her gender. Her legacy is one of faith, miracles and a pioneering spirit. We can all learn from this legacy as it points to the supernatural power of God that is available to anyone who will give Him a relentless "Yes!"

Oral Roberts

Pentecostal evangelist Oral Roberts (born Granville Oral Roberts on January 24, 1918, near Ada, Oklahoma, and died December 15, 2009, Newport Beach, California) is known for his faith-healing television ministry.

The fifth and youngest child of a desperately poor Pentecostal preacher and farmer, Roberts suffered a nearly fatal case of tuberculosis as a teenager and failed to finish high school. In 1935 he had a conversion experience in which he believed that he was miraculously healed. Three years later he married Evelyn Lutman Fahnestock, a preacher's daughter. He spent twelve years as a pastor in several towns in the South and built up his own organization, the Pentecostal Holiness Church. He studied at Oklahoma Baptist College (1943–45) and other religious universities part-time.[3]

Oral Roberts changed the landscape of healing evangelism during his time. Many were saved and healed during his tent revivals. He was one of the first to preach on the "prosperity gospel," which teaches "that God desires temporal happiness and security for his faithful and rewards devotion and generous tithing or donations with financial wealth and other blessings," and as "a groundbreaking televangelist, Roberts mentored a number of younger ministers who went on to have television and multimedia empires of their own."[4]

Oral Roberts was and still remains a legend in charismatic Christianity and Christianity as a whole. I remember watching a clip where he ministered to a boy who was born crippled. I will never forget how patient he was when praying for the young man. There was a peculiar anointing on his life and ministry. You couldn't watch him and change the channel. There was a pull. There was a captivation. When I met his son many years ago, I asked him to pray over me that I would receive a mantle of healing similar to that of his father, one I believe that I have received.

Jack G. Coe

Jack G. Coe (1918–1956) was born in Oklahoma City, Oklahoma, to Christian parents who were not churchgoers. George, his father, was an alcoholic with a gambling addiction. George had Christian parents, but they were not able change their son's ways. "When Jack was five his father gambled away all their furniture and their house, leaving his mother Blanche destitute with seven children."[5] This made Jack's childhood challenging, to say the least. Enduring many trials and tribulations, Jack eventually yielded to the call of God upon his life and years later met and married his beautiful wife.

> In 1946 God spoke to Coe and his wife Juanita to sell their house and start an itinerant ministry. They purchased a beat up truck and a ministry tent and began to live on the road. In 1948 God spoke to Coe to go to Redding, California. A woman, whose leg was about to be amputated, was healed and the news spread throughout the city. God blessed the couple, and for the first time [they] had enough money to be ahead on their finances. Healings and miracles regularly occurred in his meetings . . . as he challenged people to believe God.[6]

Jack Coe was known for a dramatic and unorthodox style of healing evangelism. Reminiscent of his predecessor Smith Wigglesworth, he believed in being very aggressive when it came to dealing with sickness and diseases. Even though Coe was controversial at the time of his ministry, he saw many healings and deliverances as he preached. What I like about Jack Coe is his audacious faith. He did not possess the refined sophistication of Oral Roberts. When I would read about him throughout my earlier years in ministry, it would cause me to believe that I could be audacious as well. Thank you, Brother Coe, for showing us what it means to be fearless.

Kathryn Kuhlman

Kathryn Johanna Kuhlman was born in Concordia, Missouri, on May 9, 1907. By the time of her death in Tulsa, Oklahoma, on

February 20, 1976, "millions counted her as their minister, and thousands claimed that they had experienced her healing powers."

Kuhlman's career in evangelism began at the age of seventeen while visiting her sister Myrtle Parrott, wife of the Sedalia-born Everett Parrott. Both Myrtle and Everett had attended Moody Bible Institute and were evangelizing the West. Myrtle persuaded Kuhlman's mother, Emma Walkenhorst Kuhlman, to allow Kathryn to travel with them for a short period. When the time came for Kathryn to return home, she chose to stay with her sister and brother-in-law and soon found herself at the altar giving her testimony and ministering to those who responded to Everett's message.

At the age of twenty-one, in 1928, Kuhlman began her own ministry.[7]

In the 1930s, she had a pioneering radio show called *Smiling Through*, and she went on to create the Christian talk-show format with her nationally syndicated show, *I Believe in Miracles*, which began in 1965. In some five hundred episodes, she interviewed people who had received healing through her ministry. Kuhlman "denied that she was a 'faith healer,' claiming that healing was produced by the Holy Spirit; her gift was in recognizing the healing."[8]

One pastor who witnessed the many healings at a Kuhlman crusade observed the following:

Spontaneously, and quite suddenly, enormously powerful miracles were happening all over the large convention center. A woman with a large mass on her neck on the front row was instantly healed—the mass simply disappeared. People were leaving wheelchairs behind and walking for the first time in years.[9]

Kuhlman claimed, "I believe God's first choice for this ministry was a man, his second choice, too. But no man was willing to pay the price. I was just naïve enough to say, 'Take nothing, and use it.' And He has been doing that ever since."[10]

No one has impacted my understanding of the Holy Spirit and desire to go deeper in intimacy with Him than Kathryn Kuhlman. Despite the challenges she faced and mistakes that she made, I can still hear her say, *Don't grieve the Holy Spirit. Don't you know He is all I got!* There was a radical dependency on the Holy Spirit that characterized her ministry. There was a purity and sincerity in her voice that you immediately could tell was genuine. She helped me to understand that the Holy Spirit is a Person, not a "Something" or an "It." Rather, He is the third Person of the Trinity, who desires to commune with me daily. I want to be so close to the Holy Spirit that I can say what Kathryn Kuhlman said: "Don't you know He is all I got!"

Bill Johnson

Bill Johnson is a fifth-generation pastor with a rich heritage in the Holy Spirit. Bill and his wife, Brenda (Beni), are the senior pastors of Bethel Church, in Redding, California. Together they serve a growing number of churches that have partnered for revival. This leadership network has crossed denominational lines, building relationships that enable church leaders to walk successfully in both purity and power. All three of their children and spouses are involved in full-time ministry. They also have nine wonderful grandchildren.

The first time I was exposed to Bill Johnson's ministry was when I became a published author. One of Pastor Bill's earlier books, *When Heaven Invades Earth*, was a transformational teaching for me. He expressed a theology of the Holy Spirit as more than just a concept or an idea, but an abiding Friend who connects us deeply to the heart of God.

Years ago, God gave me a prophetic dream about Bill Johnson and his church. At the time, I had never even seen Bethel Church before. God showed me the church parking lot, church building, auditorium and surrounding communities. I went into the church, and as I was walking into the auditorium, Bill Johnson walked out and said, "Hello, man of God!" He walked toward a chair and sat down and began to worship God passionately. I woke up from the dream with a deep sense that he was a man who loved and knew how to abide in the presence of God. His books and teachings have mentored me in many ways and imparted in me a love for Revival Culture, as well as a reverence and passion for the presence of God.

At one point, I wanted to be the Black Bill Johnson, until God quickly reminded me that He didn't want me to be anything other than the person He created. I am grateful for the life and ministry of Bill Johnson. I believe that God raises up generals in every generation whom He anoints with a unique gifting to show us an aspect of His heart and character that we need to experience the move of God in that generation; Bill Johnson is one of those special gifts to our generation.

Joan Hunter

Joan Hunter has been involved in the healing ministry for over thirty years. Along with her parents, the late Charles and Frances Hunter (the "Happy Hunters"), she has ministered to thousands of people in the area of physical healings. She has traveled the world, laying hands on the sick and seeing them recover. God has expanded her ministry to include total healing—body, soul and spirit. Joan is married to Kelley Murrell and lives in Pinehurst, Texas. She has four grown daughters, her husband has four sons, and she is a grandmother.

Joan co-pastored a church in Dallas for eighteen years until 1999, giving her a wide range of experience in the ministry. She is also the author of *Healing the Whole Man Handbook*. God has healed Joan in every area of her life. She encourages others that they can lay hands on the sick and see them recover. The healing power of God is not reserved for just a few, but for those who believe. Joan encourages you not to give up on your dreams and visions, but to fulfill the destiny that God has for you.

Years ago, I was going through one of the most difficult financial times of my life. My wife and I couldn't afford to "pay attention." The Lord brought me one of Joan Hunter's books. This message changed my life. Even though my wife had copies of *To Heal the Sick* by Charles and Frances Hunter for years, I had never read a single page. This particular book, however, was transformational to my mindset at the time.

One day, I received a phone call from Joan; we immediately connected and have been friends ever since. During one of our meetings, she prayed for my wife, Gloria, who at the time was having back problems, and Gloria was instantly healed. I believe in impartation, and I also believe that I have received much impartation through Joan Hunter's ministry. I have witnessed Vietnam veterans be totally healed and restored from PTSD through her ministry. I have witnessed broken women be totally restored after abuse and trauma, and I have witnessed those in chronic pain for decades experience complete healing and deliverance. Sometimes God allows us to come across people whose ministries have impacted us more substantially than we realize and whose impact will not be completely felt until much later, but I know that Joan Hunter is a general in the faith and a torch lighter in the ministry of healing.

Sid Roth

Sid Roth, a former account executive for Merrill Lynch, was raised in a traditional Jewish home. Yet religious tradition provided no answers when he hit rock bottom in 1972. With his life out of control and his marriage in shambles, Sid was set free from demonic oppression through a supernatural encounter with Jesus. Immediately, he began to boldly proclaim Jesus as the Jewish Messiah, even appearing on Kathryn Kuhlman's television show,

I Believe in Miracles, shortly after he was featured on the front page of a Washington, DC, newspaper.[11] He is a pioneer in the convergence of Jews and Christians in Messiah Jesus. His television program, *It's Supernatural!*, documents miracles and is viewed internationally.

The first book I ever wrote was a book about healing called *Possessing Your Healing*, and this book somehow found itself into the hands of Sid Roth. He has spent years investigating the supernatural and introducing the charismatic Christian world to the greatest gifts to the body of Christ. He read my book from cover to cover and invited me on his television show. The rest is history. His ministry has provoked a desire in me for the supernatural that cannot even be explained. Today, we are partners and friends.

It is often hard to recognize the deep significance that someone has to the Body of Christ when they are someone you are very close to, but I would be remiss if I didn't take this opportunity to acknowledge the impact that Sid Roth has made in my life personally and in the lives of millions of people. I actually remember the first time Sid Roth and I had a very deep conversation; it was after God had given me a word of knowledge about his life. This sparked a deeper conversation, which led to a deeper friendship. I have had the privilege of serving on his board of directors, but the greatest blessing has been the opportunity to witness a man of impeccable character and integrity.

Sid Roth's love for the supernatural is only rivaled by his love for his family and his unwavering love for the Jewish people. He has led more Jews to Christ in crusade-style meetings than the apostle led to Christ on the Day of Pentecost. I personally witnessed one thousand Russian Jews come to faith in Messiah in one meeting. I believe that Sid Roth is an apostle to his generation and that the anointing on his life has fostered a fresh love for the supernatural, and for the Jewish people, in the hearts of millions of believers all over the world.

Randy Clark

Randy Clark is an international speaker who holds a D.Min. from United Theological Seminary and an M.Div. from Southern Baptist Theological Seminary. He is the founder of Global Awakening, "a teaching, healing, and impartation ministry that crosses denominational lines" (www.globalawakening.com) and is part of the Apostolic Network of Global Awakening. He travels extensively for conferences, international missions, leadership training and humanitarian aid. Dr. Clark and his wife, DeAnne, are based in Pennsylvania.

The first time I heard the story of Dr. Randy Clark, I was watching a video where he recounted his experience being prayed for by Dr. Rodney Howard-Browne, who was so frustrated that Dr. Clark kept coming through the line that he pushed him down. His gentle demeanor, biblical scholarship and simple yet profound exposition of the Word of God have been a blessing to the Body of Christ. More than that is the fact that he has a powerful healing ministry, where he not only teaches people about divine healing but also activates them to go out and heal the sick.

Dr. Clark has pioneered an approach to Revival Culture and the supernatural that is both practically and theologically grounded. It is not often that you find a love for the Word of God and the move of the Spirit so powerfully expressed in one person. Many have been healed and touched by the power of God through his crusades, training schools and seminars all over the world. He has written several must-read books on healing today (for example, *The Essential Guide to Healing* by Randy Clark and Bill Johnson) and has established a platform to equip healing ministers all over the world. Through his Christian Healing Certification program, many have been equipped with greater faith and boldness to pray for the sick.

Though I have not personally gone through his certification program, his teachings have had a great impact on the way we pray for the sick. I have seen thousands healed by the power of God, and I believe that generals such as Dr. Clark should be credited for the impact they have made on the future of the Church.

I believe that those who have gone before us, as well as those who are still here, are a vital part of the next great move of God in this generation. Their teachings, impartations and deposits have left an indelible mark on our generation and have acted as a standard of excellence in life and ministry.

SUMMARY QUESTIONS

1. What should we learn from the generals of the faith who have gone before us?
2. How do the testimonies of various heroes of the faith demonstrate bold faith and perseverance?
3. How do the lives and legacies of these generals of the faith teach us to have an intimate relationship with the Holy Spirit?

MIRACLE ACTIVATION

Father, I thank You for Your power and presence in my life. I thank You that Your grace is working effectually in and through me to release the Kingdom of God into my sphere of influence in a way that brings Your name glory and transforms the lives of Your people. I declare that I release miracles everywhere I go. I declare that lives are changed and healed through Your power working in me. I declare that Your Spirit flows through my gifts to touch people in a tangible way. I will not yield to fear, but instead, I yield to the supernatural faith You have given to me. I declare that miracles, signs and wonders are easy to me because they are my spiritual inheritance in Christ. I will take the things that I have learned in this book, implement them into my spiritual life and experience accelerated growth as a result. In the name of Jesus, Amen!

Conclusion

As I conclude this book, my prayer is that the Holy Spirit will take every biblical principle contained herein and deposit it into your heart, and that it would yield lasting godly fruit. As you consider the reality walking in the supernatural power of God daily, I want you to ponder and meditate on the truths that I have shared in *Releasing Miracles*. I believe God wants you to live a supernatural life. I believe God is calling you to a life of victory and breakthrough. I challenge you to step out of the boat and walk on water.

I believe that the Holy Spirit is calling us into a deeper level of communion and devotion to Him. This spiritual awakening will create a culture in our churches where the miraculous power of God will be as normal as breathing. May our theology be undergirded by our "kneeology," and our passion demonstrated with power. The Kingdom of God is real and substantial, and it is high time that the Church carry the proof of the resurrection of Jesus Christ—not only in our preaching and teaching, but also in our love and our works.

As you ponder the truths that I have shared, my prayer is that the Word of God will come alive on the inside of you and that you will see the manifestation of the glory of God in your life. The world is waiting for the sons of God to be made apparent. Don't fear. The Holy Spirit desires to flow through you for His glory. Get ready to release miracles today!

Acknowledgments

I want to acknowledge my Lord and Savior, Jesus Christ, who is the source of everything good in my life and the One who enabled me to write this and all of my books.

I want to acknowledge my beautiful wife, Gloria. You are my best friend and greatest partner in life and ministry.

I want to acknowledge my five children: Ella, Naomi, Isaac, Israel and Anna. Daddy loves you more than you could ever imagine. Everything I have done is for you.

I want to acknowledge my staff for helping me with this book. I also want to acknowledge David Sluka and the entire Baker Publishing Group/Chosen Books team for believing in me and this message and for all the time and resources you have invested in this book. Thank you!

I want to acknowledge my church family (Grace & Peace Global Fellowship) and my pastor, Wayne C. Thompson, for all that you have imparted into me.

Finally, I want to acknowledge the generals of the faith who have paved the way for this message to the body of Christ; I honor and salute you!

Notes

Chapter 1 Miracles

1. "Bethesda," *Easton's Bible Dictionary*, Bible Study Tools, https://www.bible studytools.com/dictionary/bethesda/.

2. All definitions of Greek and Hebrew terms are from the sources available at https://www.blueletterbible.org, including *Strong's Concordance*, Larry Pierce's *Outline of Biblical Usage*, and *Thayer's Greek Lexicon*.

3. This and all subsequent definitions of English words, unless otherwise cited, are from Oxford University Press, available at https://www.lexico.com.

4. "Inheritance," *Merriam-Webster*, Merriam-Webster, https://www.merriam -webster.com/dictionary/inheritance.

Chapter 2 Jesus: The Blueprint of the Miraculous

1. Luke 5:20.

2. Verses 23–24.

Chapter 3 Understanding Biblical Faith: There's No Manifestation without the Manifester

1. Gloria Gaither and Bill Gaither, "Because He Lives" (Gaither Copyright Management, 1971).

Chapter 7 The Power of Proclamation: Open Mouth, Open Heaven

1. Matthew 8:10, 13.

Chapter 8 Breaking Free from Guilt and Shame: Overcoming the Theology of Unworthiness

1. The rest of the "parable of the unforgiving servant" can be found in Matthew 18:21–35.

Chapter 12 How to Maintain the Miraculous: Keeping a Heart Focused on Jesus

1. Bill Johnson, "Bill Johnson: Naturally Supernatural," *Charisma* News, May 27, 2012, https://www.charismanews.com/opinion/33485-bill-johnson-naturally -supernatural.

Chapter 13 Ready, Set, Go: Practical Steps in the Miraculous

1. Carlis L. Moody Jr., "I'm Available to You," performed by Milton Brunson and The Thompson Community Singers (Warner Chappell Music, Inc.), https://www .lyrics.com/lyric/2694408/Rev.+Milton+Brunson/I%27m+Available+to+You.

Chapter 14 Heroes in the Miraculous: We Didn't Get Here on Our Own

1. Gilbert King, "The Incredible Disappearing Evangelist," *Smithsonian*, June 17, 2013, https://www.smithsonianmag.com/history/the-incredible-disappearing -evangelist-572829/.

2. King, "The Incredible Disappearing Evangelist."

3. Melissa Petruzzello, "Oral Roberts," *Encyclopedia Britannica*, February 11, 2022, https://www.britannica.com/biography/Oral-Roberts.

4. Petruzzello, "Oral Roberts."

5. "God's Healing Power," Healing and Revival Press, https://healingandrevival .com/BioJCoe.htm.

6. "God's Healing Power."

7. State Historical Society of Missouri, "Kathryn J. Kuhlman (1907–1976)," *Missouri Encyclopedia*, https://missouriencyclopedia.org/people/kuhlman-kathryn-j.

8. "Kathryn J. Kuhlman (1907–1976)."

9. Rob Granger, "Founders of Our Faith: Kathryn Kuhlman," *Escondido Times-Advocate*, September 13, 2020, https://www.times-advocate.com/articles/founders -of-our-faith-kathryn-kuhlman.

10. Kathryn Kuhlman with Jamie Buckingham, *A Glimpse into Glory* (Newberry, FL: Bridge-Logos, 1983), 27.

11. "Sid Roth on 'I Believe in Miracles,'" Sid Roth's *It's Supernatural!*, https:// www.sidroth.org/sid-roth-believe-miracles/.

Dr. Kynan Bridges is the senior pastor of Grace & Peace Global Fellowship in Tampa, Florida. A highly sought-after speaker and published author of several books, Dr. Bridges is known for his dynamic teaching ministry and practical approach to applying the deep truths of the Word of God. He's appeared on numerous media outlets, including Daystar, Sid Roth's *It's Supernatural!*, FaithTV, CTN, Cornerstone and TCT. He and his wife, Gloria, have five children and reside in Tampa. Learn more at kynanbridges.com.